FINBOROUGH | THEATRE

By special arrangement with Samuel French Ltd

Mercurius in association with Neil McPherson for the Finborough Theatre presents

The first professional UK production in nearly 40 years

THE BIOGRAPH GIRL

Book by Warner Brown
Lyrics by Warner Brown and David Heneker
Music by David Heneker

FINBOROUGH | THEATRE
VIBRANT **NEW WRITING** | UNIQUE **REDISCOVERIES**

The production commissioned by the Finborough Theatre as part of their 'Celebrating British Music Theatre' series.
First performance at The Gardner Centre, Brighton: Tuesday, 21 October 1980.
First performance at the Phoenix Theatre: Wednesday, 19 November 1980.
First performance at the Finborough Theatre: Tuesday, 22 May 2018.

THE BIOGRAPH GIRL

Book by Warner Brown
Lyrics by Warner Brown and David Heneker
Music by David Heneker

Cast in order of speaking
Lillian	**Emily Langham**
Dorothy	**Lauren Chinery**
Momma	**Nova Skipp**
Mary	**Sophie Linder-Lee**
D. W. Griffith	**Jonathan Leinmuller**
Epping	**Joshua C. Jackson**
Rose	**Charlie Ryall**
Bitzer	**Jason Morell**
Zukor	**Jason Morell**
Sennett	**Matthew Cavendish**
Man of the South	**Joshua C. Jackson**
Spec	**Harry Haden-Brown**

The action takes place in various locations in New York City and Hollywood from 1912–1928.

The performance lasts approximately two hours.

There will be one interval of fifteen minutes.

Director	**Jenny Eastop**
Musical Director	**Harry Haden-Brown**
Choreographer	**Holly Hughes**
Dance Captain	**Emily Langham**
Designer	**Anna Yates**
Lighting Designer	**Ali Hunter**
Stage Manager	**Riddell Erridge**
Producer	**Bradley Benson**

Our patrons are respectfully reminded that, in this intimate theatre, any noise such as rustling programmes, talking or the ringing of mobile phones may distract the actors and your fellow audience-members.

We regret there is no admittance or re-admittance to the auditorium whilst the performance is in progress.

Interval drinks may be ordered in advance at the bar.

MUSICAL NUMBERS

Act One

The Moving Picture Show	Company
Workin' In Flickers	Mary
The Moment I Close My Eyes	Griffith
Diggin' Gold Dust	Company
Every Lady	Lillian/Griffith/Bitzer
I Just Wanted To Make Him Laugh	Sennett/Lillian
They Don't Call 'Em Flickers	Company
Rivers of Blood	Man of the South
I Like To Be The Way I Am In My Own Front Parlour	
	Mary/Publicists/Pressmen
Beyond Babel	Griffith/Company

Act Two

A David Griffith Show	Company
More Than A Man	Lillian
I Like To Be The Way I Am (reprise)	Mary
The Industry	Rose/Company
Gentle Fade	Griffith
One Long Party	Rose/Company
The Biograph Girl	Mary/Company
One Of The Pioneers	Griffith
Put It In The Tissue Paper	Sennett/Mary/Lillian
Workin' In Flickers (reprise)	Company

Music for *Every Lady* and *I Just Wanted to Make Him Laugh* by Warner Brown and David Heneker

Matthew Cavendish |Sennett
Trained at LAMDA.
Theatre includes *Showstopper!* (Lyric Theatre) the original Broadway cast of *The Play That Goes Wrong* (Lyceum Theatre, New York City), *The Play That Goes Wrong* (Duchess Theatre) *Peter Pan Goes Wrong* (Apollo Theatre and National Tour), *Lights! Camera! Improvise!* (Edinburgh Festival), *Sleeping Beauty* (Park Theatre), *The Boys From Syracuse* (Union Theatre), *The Borrowers*, winner of the TMA Best Children's Show (Northern Stage, Newcastle), *An Intimate Evening with Ruthie Henshall* (Apex Theatre, Suffolk) and *News Revue* (Canal Café Theatre).
Television includes *A Christmas Carol Goes Wrong*.
Matt is a member of both the Olivier and Tony award winning companies Mischief Theatre and Showstopper – *The Improvised Musical*.

Lauren Chinery | Dorothy Gish
Trained at Performance Preparation Academy, Guildford.
Theatre includes *Miss Nightingale* (London Hippodrome), *Beauty and the Beast* (Cast, Doncaster), *Dreamboats and Petticoats* (National Tour), *Gatsby* (Leicester Square Theatre) and *Can't Stop It* (London Theatre Workshop).

Joshua C. Jackson | Epping
Trained at The Arts Educational School London.
Theatre includes *Caliban* (Orange Tree Theatre, Richmond), *The Motherf**ker With the Hat* and *Icarus's Mother* (Andrew Lloyd Webber Theatre), *Keeping It Real* (Edinburgh Festival) and *Showstoppers the Improvised Musical*.
Television and Film includes *Autopsy*, *Black Mirror* and *American Animals*.
Commercials include *Apple* and *Knorr*.

Emily Langham | Lillian Gish
Trained at Arts Educational Schools having been awarded an Andrew Lloyd Webber Scholarship. Theatre includes *Follies* (National Theatre), *Mrs Henderson Presents* (Royal Alexandra Theatre, Toronto), *Cats* (UK and European Tour), *Mack and Mabel* (Chichester Festival Theatre and National Tour) and *Les Misérables* (Queen's Theatre).
Television includes *Help*, *Stupid* and *Dead Ringers*.
Radio includes *Friday Night is Music Night*.
Workshops include *A Theory of Justice: The Musical* and *Absolute Hell* (National Theatre).

Sophie Linder-Lee | Mary Pickford
Trained at Performers College where she was the winner of the Music Award and Third Year Award.
Theatre includes *Big Fish* (The Other Palace), *The Rocky Horror Show* (Italian Tour and Oxford Playhouse), *The Rocky Horror Show* (National Tour) and the 42nd anniversary gala performance of *Rocky Horror Live* (Playhouse Theatre), *Wicked* (Apollo Victoria Theatre), *Mamma Mia* (Prince of Wales Theatre), *Silence! The Musical* (Barons Court Theatre), *Apollo Victoria 80th Anniversary Gala* (Apollo Victoria Theatre), *P and O Cruises* (Stadium Theatre Company), *Broadway's Spirit of Christmas* (US Tour), *Jack and the Beanstalk* and *Cinderella* (Towngate Theatre, Basildon) and *Cinderella* (QDOS).
Film includes *Rocky Horror Live* and *Mamma Mia! The Movie* (pre-production workshop).
Television includes dancer on *The X Factor* with *Mamma Mia!*, *The Slammer*, *Top of the Pops* and *Halifax* commercial.
Recordings include *Don't Stop Believing* (National Tour).
www.sophielinderlee.com

Jonathan Leinmuller | D. W. Griffith
Trained at Drama Centre London.
Theatre includes *Lucky Stiff* (Union Theatre), *Domestic Extremists* (The Space), *A Bright Room Called Day* (Southwark Playhouse), *Innovation* (Park Theatre), *Darling of the Day* (Union Theatre), *Billy Budd* (Southwark Playhouse), *Little Baby Nothing* (Theatre503), *Paradise* (Arcola Theatre), *Pericles* (Rose Theatre) and *Elegant Fowl* (Old Red Lion Theatre).
Film includes *Latitude the Movie*.
Television includes *Argentine Tango*.

Jason Morell | Bitzer and Zukor
Trained at the Central School of Speech and Drama
Theatre includes *Present Laughter* (Theatre Royal Bath), *The Merchant of Venice, The Taming of the Shrew* (Royal Shakespeare Company), *Oliver!* (Theatre Royal, Drury Lane), *Faustus*; (Hampstead Theatre), *The Prince and the Pauper* (Unicorn Theatre), *Lysistrata* (Arcola), *Rainsnakes* (The Young Vic), *The Reckless are Dying Out, The Cenci* (Lyric Theatre, Hammersmith); *The Critic* (Manchester Royal Exchange), *Ritual in Blood* (Nottingham Playhouse), *The Duchess of Malfi, Romeo and Juliet, The Double Inconstancy, The Rehearsal* (Salisbury Playhouse), *The Silver Lake* (Wilton's Music Hall), *Swan White* (Gate Theatre), *The Artificial Jungle* (Leicester Haymarket), *The Leonardo Project, The Cutting of the Cloth, The Difficult Man* (National Theatre Studio), *Hamlet* (Cheek by Jowl, National and International Tour) and *Gertrude, the Cry, Thirteen Objects* (The Wrestling School at Riverside Studios and Elsinore Castle).
Film includes *Photocopier, Secret Love, The Lake, The Gathering, Mrs Brown, Wilde, Biddy, Princess and Damage*.
Television includes *Doctor Who, Affinity, Ultimate Force, My Dad's the Prime Minister, Hear the Silence, Second Sight, Aristophanes, The Gods are Laughing, The Bill* and *J'Accuse Agatha*.

Charlie Ryall | Rose
Trained at Stella Adler Studio of Acting.
Theatre includes *The Bashful Lover* and *The Elder Brother* (Sam Wanamaker Playhouse), *NewsRevue* (Canal Café Theatre), *The Feigned Courtesans*, *The Alchemist* and *The Devil is an Ass* (Rose Theatre), *Bugsy Malone* (Civic Hall, Stratford-upon-Avon), *Much Ado About Nothing* (New Wimbledon Theatre), *King Lear* (Cockpit Theatre), *Macbeth* (Lion and Unicorn Theatre), *Hamlet* (Royal Shakespeare Company), *The Importance of Being Earnest* (Brighton Festival), *Buchwald and Friends! A Victoria Wood Revue* (Leicester Square Theatre) and *Joseph and the Amazing Technicolor Dreamcoat* (New London Theatre and National Tour)
Film includes *Harry Potter and the Deathly Hallows Part II*.
Television includes *First Men in the Moon*, *Jake's Progress* and *A Touch of Frost*.

Nova Skipp | Momma
Trained at the Arts Educational Schools, London.
Theatre includes *Aspects of Love* (Prince of Wales Theatre), *The Phantom of the Opera* (Her Majesty's Theatre), *Salad Days* (Vaudeville Theatre and National Tour), *Chess in Concert* (Royal Albert Hall), *The Sound of Music* (London Palladium), *Assassins* (Pleasance London), *Follies, Meet Me in St Louis, Damn Yankees* (Landor Theatre), *Apartment 40C* (The Other Palace), *Anything Goes* (Upstairs at the Gatehouse). *Gentlemen Prefer Blondes, Annie, The King and I, Acorn Antiques, The Two Most Perfect Things, Abigail's Party, Carrie's War, The Smallest Show on Earth* and *Funny Girl* (National Tours), *Cats* (Stuttgart), *The Sound of Music* (Crucible Theatre, Sheffield), *Kes* (Theatre Royal York and Derby Theatre), *A Midsummer Night's Dream, Troilus* and *Cressida* (Open Air Theatre, Regent's Park), *Oklahoma!, The Rise and Fall of Little Voice, Bedroom Farce* and *Carousel* (Octagon Theatre, Yeovil), *Carousel* (Perth Theatre, Scotland), *The Rocky Horror Show, Grease* (Gaiety Theatre, Isle of Man), *Side by Side by Sondheim* and *Annie* (Gordon Craig Theatre, Stevenage), *Pardon Me, Prime Minister* and *Hay Fever* (Theatre Royal Windsor).
Recordings include *His Excellency, Once Upon a Dream* and *Children's Musical Theatre*.
www.novaskipp.com

Warner Brown | Book and Lyrics
Playwright and lyricist Warner Brown works on both sides of the Atlantic. As a bookwriter and lyricist, he has collaborated with the composers Angelo Badalamenti, Michael Feinstein, Tony Hatch, David Heneker, Michael Reed, Jimmy Roberts, Joshua Schmidt, Jim Steinman, Charles Strouse, George David Weiss and, by permission of the Cole Porter Trusts, the late Cole Porter. His work in the UK and London includes *Son Of A Preacher Man* (current UK National Tour), *Cinderella* (London Palladium), *Six For Gold* and *The Black and White Ball* (King's Head Theatre), the play *The Prospero Suite* (Everyman Theatre, Cheltenham), *The House On The Corner* (Edinburgh Festival) and the New Version of *Half A Sixpence*. Work in Europe and the US includes *Garbo – The Musical and Flickers*. For BBC Worldwide and Global Creatures, Warner wrote the arena show *Walking With Dinosaurs – the Arena Spectacular*, which has won many international awards, including the Billboard Magazine Creative Content Award. Warner has extensive writing credits for the BBC and was Script Associate of the BBC Classic Musicals series, for which he adapted fourteen musicals and directed such artists as Anthony Newley, Barbara Cook and Tyne Daly. He is co-sponsor of The S&S Award for new musical theatre writing.

David Heneker | Music and Lyrics
David Heneker (1906-2001) began his songwriting career with such wartime classics as *Bang Goes The Drum*, *There's A New World Over The Skyline* and *The Thing-Ummy Bob*. He went on to write a series of classic West End musicals including *Expresso 3 Bongo* (Saville Theatre, with Wolf Mankowitz and Monty Norman), which was later made into a film starring Laurence Harvey and Cliff Richard, *Irma La Douce* (West End and Broadway, with Monty Norman and Julian More), *Make Me An Offer* (New Theatre, with Wolf Mankowitz and Monty Norman), which won the Evening Standard Award for Best New Musical, *Half A Sixpence* (West End and Broadway, with Beverley Cross, starring Tommy Steele), which was filmed in 1967 and revived in 2007 and 2016. *Half A Sixpence* won Tony nominations for Best Musical and Best Original Score. *Charlie Girl* (Adelphi Theatre, with John Taylor), which ran in the West End for five years, followed; then Jorrocks (New Theatre, with Beverley Cross), *Phil the Fluter* (Palace Theatre, with Beverley Cross), *The Amazons* (Nottingham Playhouse, with Michael Stewart), *Popkiss* (Globe Theatre, with John Addison and Michael Ashton)

and *Peg* (Phoenix Theatre, with Ronald Millar). David was the first British writer to have two shows on Broadway which ran for more than five hundred performances.

Jenny Eastop | Director
Productions at the Finborough Theatre include *Mr Gillie* for which she received an OffWestEnd nomination for Best Director. Jenny is the Artistic Director of Mercurius Theatre for which she has directed *The Waiting Room* (Leicester Square Theatre and Above the Arts), *The Alchemist*, *The Devil Is An Ass*, *A Chaste Maid in Cheapside* and *A Trick to Catch the Old One* (Rose Theatre, Bankside), *Anton Chekhov's Vaudevilles* (Jermyn Street Theatre) and *School for Wives* (White Bear Theatre) for which she received an OffWestEnd nomination for Best Director. Jenny has also directed for Shakespeare's Globe, National Theatre Studio and London New Play Festival, including the premiere of Peter Nichols' play *So Long Life* (The Tobacco Factory, Bristol), *Warde Street* (Park Theatre) for which she received an OffWestEnd nomination for Best Director, and *Henna Night* (Leicester Square Theatre).
Jenny has worked as Associate Director to Michael Blakemore on *The Life* which won four OffWestEnd Awards including Best Musical Production (Southwark Playhouse), *Blithe Spirit* (Gielgud Theatre and US Tour), *Embers* (Duke of York's Theatre), *Democracy* (National Theatre, Wyndham's Theatre, Broadway, and Sydney Theatre Company), *Afterlife* (National Theatre) and *Three Sisters* (Playhouse Theatre).
Resident Direction includes working with Roger Michell on *Blue/Orange* (Duchess Theatre) and *The Homecoming* (National Theatre) and Matthew Warchus on *The Devil Is an Ass* (Royal Shakespeare Company).

Harry Haden-Brown | Musical Director
Productions at the Finborough Theatre include *Adding Machine: The Musical*.
Trained at the University of Bristol and with National Youth Music Theatre.
Theatre includes *West End Wired* (Bristol Hippodrome), *Cinderella* (Grand Pavilion, Porthcawl), *Gate* (Cockpit Theatre), *Drink Up Thy Cider* (Redgrave Theatre, Bristol), *Side by Side by Sondheim* (Bristol Hippodrome), *Ophelia* (National Tour), *Half a Sixpence* (McMillan Theatre, Bridgwater), *Carrie* (The Loco Klub, Bristol), *Jack and the Beanstalk* (Grand Pavilion, Porthcawl), *The 25th Annual Putnam County Spelling Bee* (Alma Tavern,

Bristol), *Fiddler on the Roof* (Bristol Hippodrome), *[title of show]* (Edinburgh Festival), *Thoroughly Modern Millie* (McMillan Theatre, Bridgwater), *Into The Woods* (Olympus Theatre, Bristol, and Winston Theatre, Bristol), *Dogfight* (The Pegg Studio Theatre, Bristol) and *Cabaret* (Bristol Bierkellar). Assistant Musical Direction or/Keys include *My Fair Lady* (Bristol Hippodrome), *Sunset Boulevard* (Bristol Hippodrome), *Pendragon* (Theatre Royal Bury St Edmunds), *Lakme* (National Tour and Swansea City Opera), *The Juniper Tree* (UK premiere - Hammond Theatre), *La Boheme* (National Tour and Swansea City Opera), *Snow White* (Bristol Hippodrome), *Girlfriends* (The Tunnels, Bristol), *How to Succeed in Business Without Really Trying* (Wilton's Music Hall) and *Harley's Place* (Royal Academy of Music Workshop).
Harry is house Musical Director for *The Secret Cabaret* and *Broadway Sessions UK*.

Holly Hughes | Choreographer
Trained at The Arts Educational Schools, London.
Acting includes *HMS Pinafore* (Battersea Barge), *Carousel* (Broadway Theatre, Catford), *Mother Goose* (Northcott Theatre, Exeter), *Aladdin* (Broadway Theatre, Peterborough), *My Fair Lady* (Aberystwyth Arts Centre), *Babes in the Wood* (Pomegranate Theatre, Chesterfield), *Babe, the Sheep Pig* (Open Air Theatre, Regents Park), *The Untold Story* (National Trust) and *The Horse of the Year Show* (Olympia).
Associate and Assistant Choreography includes *West Side Story* (Royal Northern College of Music), *HMS Pinafore* (Battersea Barge and King's Head Theatre), *Carousel* (Broadway Theatre, Catford), *Once Upon A Time At The Adelphi* (Union Theatre), *Moonshadow* (Workshop), *My Favorite Year* (Guildhall School of Music and Drama), *The Night of 1000 Voices* (Royal Albert Hall) and *I Sing!* (Union Theatre).
Choreography includes *Mack and Mabel* (Liverpool Institute for Performing Arts), *Sasha Regan's All Male Mikado* (UK Tour) *Anyone Can Whistle* (Union Theatre) and *The Mikado* (Battersea Barge).
Holly has also been Choreographer and Assistant Director on numerous pantomimes including last year's *Beauty and the Beast* (The Corn Exchange, Newbury).

Anna Yates | Designer
Productions at the Finborough Theatre include *Mr Gillie*.
Trained at Tisch School of the Arts, New York University, and

was awarded the J.S. Seidman Award for Excellence in Design. Theatre includes *Lucia Di Lammermoor* (Fulham Opera), *Tenderly* (New Wimbledon Theatre Studio), *Kafka's Quest* (Theatre for the New City, New York), *The Miser* (Brave New World Repertory, Brooklyn), *The Face on the Barroom Floor* and *Emperor Norton* (Chelsea Opera, New York), *The Dwarf* (Vertical Player Repertory, Brooklyn), *Careers for Attractive Ladies* (Sydney Festival) and *Figaro* (Curtain Call Theatre, Albany) Film includes *The Fly Room* (Woodstock Film Festival), *She Lights Up Well* (CAAMfest), and *But Not For Me*, (Brooklyn Film Festival, NewFilmmakers New York Film Festival, Virginia Film Festival, Blowup Chicago International Arthouse Film Festival and Capital City Black Film Festival) and a number of shorts and music videos in London, New York and Sydney.

Ali Hunter | Lighting Designer
Productions at the Finborough Theatre include *Gracie*.
Theatre includes *Isaac Came Home from the Mountain* (Theatre503), *Tune-D In* (The Place), *Woman Before a Glass* (Jermyn Street Theatre), *The Acid Test* (Cockpit Theatre), *Empty Beds and Moments* (Hope Theatre), *Rattlesnake* (Open Clasp Theatre Company), *Tenderly* (New Wimbledon Studio), *Katzenmusik* (Royal Court Theatre Upstairs) and *Foreign Body* (Women of the World Festival).
She was recently named Young Associate Lighting Designer for Matthew Bourne's forthcoming production.

Bradley Benson | Producer
Trained at Birmingham Ormiston Academy.
Producing includes two musical cabaret nights at the Custard Factory, Birmingham. He recently founded Bradley Benson Theatrical Productions.
Assistant Producing includes assisting Amy Anzel and Matt Chisling on *Vanities: The Musical* (Trafalgar Studios 2), the 25th anniversary production of *Moby Dick! The Musical* (Union Theatre) and *The Life* (Southwark Playhouse).
Follow @BBTPUK on Twitter.

Riddell Erridge | Stage Manager
Stage Management includes *The Crucible* (Reading University Drama Society)
She is also producing new musical *A Romantic's Guide to the Apocalypse* at the Edinburgh Festival this summer.

Production Acknowledgements
Production Photography | **Lidia Crisafulli**
Image Photographer | **Lawrence Winram ©lwinram.com**
With thanks to Richard Baker, Alison Simmons, Drama Studio London, Tom Eastop, Dorothy Eastop, Alison Oguz, Helen McAleer, Gerit Quealy, Jeremy Booth, Benjamin Garrison, Simon Bolland, Joy Blakeman, Sam Jenkins-Shaw, Renee Guest, George Ralston, Caroline Underwood, Nick Quinn, and Debbie Simmons at Samuel French.

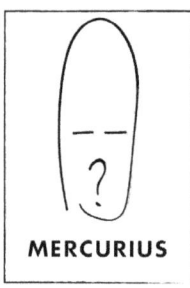

Mercurius Theatre Ltd is a limited company. Registered in England and Wales 9784123. Registered address 42 Leithcote Gardens, London SW16 2UY

The Finborough Theatre's building – including both the Finborough Arms pub and the Finborough Theatre – celebrates its 150th birthday in 2018.

Opened in 1868, the Finborough building was designed by one of the leading architects of his day, George Godwin (1813-1888) who was also the editor of the architectural magazine The Builder (which is still published today), and a sometime playwright. He is buried in nearby Brompton Cemetery.

The Finborough Arms was one of five public houses originally constructed as part of the Redcliffe Estate (which replaced the farmland and market gardens that existed before), and is one of only three pubs of the original five that still survive today.

One of the Finborough Arms' most regular customers was sanitary pioneer Thomas Crapper (1836-1910) who would would regularly begin his working day in the Finborough Arms with a bottle of champagne. His daughter, Minnie, married Ernest Finch (who was born in the flat above the theatre) of the Finch family who owned and managed the building from its opening in 1868 until the early 1930s.

FINBOROUGH | THEATRE
VIBRANT **NEW WRITING** | UNIQUE **REDISCOVERIES**

"**Probably the most influential fringe theatre in the world.**"
Time Out

"**Under Neil McPherson, possibly the most unsung of all major artistic directors in Britain, the Finborough has continued to plough a fertile path of new plays and rare revivals that gives it an influence disproportionate to its tiny 50-seat size.**"
Mark Shenton, The Stage 2017

"**The tiny but mighty Finborough**"
Ben Brantley, The New York Times

Founded in 1980 on the first floor of the building (which was previously a restaurant, a Masonic Lodge, and a billiards hall), the multi-award-winning Finborough Theatre presents plays and music theatre, concentrated exclusively on vibrant new writing and unique rediscoveries from the 19th and 20th centuries.

Our programme is unique – we never present work that has been seen anywhere in London during the last 25 years.

Do visit us our website to find out more about us, or follow us on Facebook, Twitter, Instagram, Tumblr and YouTube.

For more on the history of the building and the local area, and for full information on the Finborough Theatre's work, visit our website at **www.finboroughtheatre.co.uk**

FINBOROUGH | THEATRE

VIBRANT **NEW WRITING** | UNIQUE **REDISCOVERIES**
118 Finborough Road, London SW10 9ED
admin@finboroughtheatre.co.uk
www.finboroughtheatre.co.uk

Artistic Director | **Neil McPherson**
Founding Director | **Phil Willmott**
Resident Designer | **Alex Marker**
Executive Director | **Antonella Petrancosta**
Managing Director | **Doug Mackie**
General Managers | **Ianthe Bathurst, Katharine Edmonds** and **Nikki Hill**
Book Keeper | **Patti Williams**
Playwrights in Residence | **James Graham, Dawn King, Anders Lustgarten, Carmen Nasr, Shamser Sinha** and **Chris Thompson**
Playwrights on Attachment | **Steven Hevey, Adam Hughes, Joe Marsh, Louise Monaghan** and **Athena Stevens**
Associate Producer | **Arsalan Sattari**
Literary Manager | **Sue Healy**
Deputy Literary Manager | **Rhys Hayes**
Literary Assistants | **Hattie Collins, Ashleigh Packham** and **Charles Rogers**
Literary Assistants (International) | **Cressida Peever** and **Nick Myles**
Casting Directors | **Lucy Casson, Aurora Causin**
Board of Trustees | **Lisa Cagnacci, Felix Cassel, Gordon Hopkinson, Russell Levinson, Rebecca Maltby, Alice Pakenham, Alex Turner** and **Paul Webster**

And our many interns and volunteers.

The Finborough Theatre is a member of the Independent Theatre Council, the Society of Independent Theatres, Musical Theatre Network, The Friends of Brompton Cemetery and The Earl's Court Society; and supports #time4change's Mental Health Charter.

Supported by

Mailing
Email admin@finboroughtheatre.co.uk or give your details to our Box Office staff to join our free email list.

Feedback
We welcome your comments, complaints and suggestions. Write to Finborough Theatre, 118 Finborough Road, London SW10 9ED or email us at admin@finboroughtheatre.co.uk

Playscripts
Many of the Finborough Theatre's plays have been published and are on sale from our website.

On social media

  www.facebook.com/FinboroughTheatre

  www.twitter.com/finborough

  finboroughtheatre.tumblr.com

  www.instagram.com/finboroughtheatre

  www.youtube.com/user/finboroughtheatre

Friends
The Finborough Theatre is a registered charity. We receive no public funding, and rely solely on the support of our audiences. Please do consider supporting us by becoming a member of our Friends of the Finborough Theatre scheme. There are four categories of Friends, each offering a wide range of benefits.

Richard Tauber Friends – David and Melanie Alpers. J. D. Anderson. David Barnes. Mark Bentley. Kate Beswick. Simon Bolland. James Carroll. Deirdre Feehan. N. and D. Goldring. Loyd Grossman. Paul Guinery. David Harrison. Mary Hickson. Richard Jackson. Paul and Lindsay Kennedy. Martin and Wendy Kramer. John Lawson. Kathryn McDowall. Ghazell Mitchell. Guislaine Vincent Morland. Carol Rayman. Barry Serjent. Brian Smith. Lavinia Webb. Sandra Yarwood.
William Terriss Friends – Stuart Ffoulkes. Alan Godfrey. Ros Haigh. Melanie Johnson. Leo and Janet Liebster.
Adelaide Neilson Friends – Philip G Hooker.

Smoking is not permitted in the auditorium and the use of cameras and recording equipment is strictly prohibited.

In accordance with the requirements of the Royal Borough of Kensington and Chelsea:
1. The public may leave at the end of the performance by all doors and such doors must at that time be kept open.
2. All gangways, corridors, staircases and external passageways intended for exit shall be left entirely free from obstruction whether permanent or temporary.
3. Persons shall not be permitted to stand or sit in any of the gangways intercepting the seating or to sit in any of the other gangways.

The Finborough Theatre is licensed by the Royal Borough of Kensington and Chelsea to The Steam Industry, a registered charity and a company limited by guarantee. Registered in England and Wales no. 3448268. Registered Charity no. 1071304. Registered Office: 118 Finborough Road, London SW10 9ED.

The Steam Industry was founded by Phil Willmott in 1992. It comprises two strands to its work: the Finborough Theatre (under Artistic Director Neil McPherson); and The Phil Willmott Company (under Artistic Director Phil Willmott) which presents productions throughout London as well as annually at the Finborough Theatre.

THE BIOGRAPH GIRL

A Musical

Book by Warner Brown

Lyrics by Warner Brown and David Heneker
Music by David Heneker

samuelfrench.co.uk

Copyright © 1983, 2018 by Warner Brown, David Heneker
All Rights Reserved

THE BIOGRAPH GIRL is fully protected under the copyright laws of the British Commonwealth, including Canada, the United States of America, and all other countries of the Copyright Union. All rights, including professional and amateur stage productions, recitation, lecturing, public reading, motion picture, radio broadcasting, television and the rights of translation into foreign languages are strictly reserved.

ISBN 978-0-573-18001-9
www.samuelfrench.co.uk
www.samuelfrench.com

Artwork designed by LWPhotography Ltd. © 2018 lwinram.com

FOR AMATEUR PRODUCTION ENQUIRIES

UNITED KINGDOM AND WORLD
EXCLUDING NORTH AMERICA
plays@samuelfrench.co.uk
020 7255 4302/01

Each title is subject to availability from Samuel French, depending upon country of performance.

CAUTION: Professional and amateur producers are hereby warned that *THE BIOGRAPH GIRL* is subject to a licensing fee. Publication of this play does not imply availability for performance. Both amateurs and professionals considering a production are strongly advised to apply to the appropriate agent before starting rehearsals, advertising, or booking a theatre. A licensing fee must be paid whether the title is presented for charity or gain and whether or not admission is charged.

The professional rights in this play are controlled by The Caroline Underwood Agency, Suite 55, 88 Lower Marsh, London SE1 7AB.

No one shall make any changes in this title for the purpose of production. No part of this book may be reproduced, stored in a retrieval system, or transmitted in any form, by any means, now known or yet to be invented, including mechanical, electronic, photocopying, recording, videotaping, or otherwise, without the prior written permission of the publisher. No one shall upload this title, or part of this title, to any social media websites.

The right of Warner Brown and David Heneker to be identified as author of this work has been asserted in accordance with Section 77 of the Copyright, Designs and Patents Act 1988.

The text was correct at the time of print and may differ to what is presented on stage.

THINKING ABOUT PERFORMING A SHOW?

There are thousands of plays and musicals available to perform from Samuel French right now, and applying for a licence is easier and more affordable than you might think

From classic plays to brand new musicals, from monologues to epic dramas, there are shows for everyone.

Plays and musicals are protected by copyright law so if you want to perform them, the first thing you'll need is a licence. This simple process helps support the playwright by ensuring they get paid for their work, and means that you'll have the documents you need to stage the show in public.

Not all our shows are available to perform all the time, so it's important to check and apply for a licence before you start rehearsals or commit to doing the show.

LEARN MORE & FIND THOUSANDS OF SHOWS

Browse our full range of plays and musicals and find out more about how to license a show
www.samuelfrench.co.uk/perform

Talk to the friendly experts in our Licensing team for advice on choosing a show, and help with licensing
plays@samuelfrench.co.uk   020 7387 9373

Acting Editions
BORN TO PERFORM

Playscripts designed from the ground up to work the way you do in rehearsal, performance and study

---

Larger, clearer text for easier reading

Wider margins for notes

Performance features such as character and props lists, sound and lighting cues, and more

---

+ CHOOSE A SIZE AND STYLE TO SUIT YOU

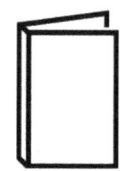 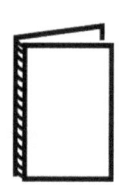 

STANDARD EDITION
Our regular paperback book at our regular size

SPIRAL-BOUND EDITION
The same size as the Standard Edition, but with a sturdy, easy-to-fold, easy-to-hold spiral-bound spine

LARGE EDITION
A4 size and spiral bound, with larger text and a blank page for notes opposite every page of text. Perfect for technical and directing use

---

| LEARN MORE | samuelfrench.co.uk/actingeditions

ABOUT THE AUTHORS

David Heneker

David Heneker's first published song was performed by Merle Oberon in the film *The Broken Melody* and his first hit was the Gracie Fields wartime classic *The Thing-Ummy Bob*. In 1948 he began performing at London's Embassy Club, in what was to become known as "David's Room". The room became a High Society hub, patronized by the likes of the Prince of Wales and Wallis Simpson. In 1958 the writer Wolf Mankowitz invited David to work with him, Monty Norman and Julian More on the score of *Expresso Bongo*, a satire of the music industry. This was first produced at the Saville Theatre starring Paul Scofield and Millicent Martin and was later made into a film starring Laurence Harvey and Cliff Richard.

From this point on, David wrote a series of classic West End and Broadway shows. *Irma la Douce*, again with Norman and More, starred Keith Michell, Elizabeth Seal and Clive Revill and was directed by Peter Brook. Transferring to Broadway, it received seven Tony nominations, including Best Musical, Miss Seal winning Best Performance by a Leading Actress in a Musical. *Make Me an Offer*, with Mankowitz and Norman once more, was directed by Joan Littlewood and won the Evening Standard Award for Best Musical. Starring Daniel Massey, the cast featured Victor Spinetti, who was later to direct *The Biograph Girl*.

David's greatest international triumph was to follow. *Half a Sixpence*, with book by Beverley Cross, starred Tommy Steele and Marti Webb, with Steele delivering a performance which has become the stuff of legend. Directed by John Dexter, the show moved to Broadway, where John Cleese played the small role of Walsingham. The show was nominated for nine Tony Awards and David became the first British writer to have two shows on Broadway running for more than 500 performances. *Half a Sixpence* was filmed in 1967, directed by George Sidney, with choreography by Gillian Lynne in her first film assignment. It was revived in 2007, starring Gary Wilmot, and 2016, starring Charlie Stemp.

In 1965 *Charlie Girl*, written with John Taylor and starring Anna Neagle, Joe Brown and Derek Nimmo, survived an initial critical roasting to run for a record 2,202 performances. It was revived in 1986, starring Cyd Charisse. *Jorrocks*, starring Joss Ackland, *The Amazons*, written with Michael Stewart, and *Popkiss*, based on the Ben Travers farce *Rookery Nook* and again starring Daniel Massey, were to follow and then came *The Biograph Girl*, written with Warner Brown. Heneker and Brown were the subjects of the BBC Two documentary *The Making of a Musical*. David's last show was *Peg* at the Phoenix Theatre, starring Sian Phillips.

Warner Brown

Warner Brown is an internationally renowned writer whose work encompasses everything from the traditional form to the radical avant-garde. He has collaborated with the composers Angelo Badalamenti, Michael Feinstein, Jenny Giering, Tony Hatch, David Heneker, Gwyneth Herbert, Michael Reed, Jimmy Roberts, Joshua Schmidt, Jim Steinman, Charles Strouse, George David Weiss and, by permission of the Cole Porter Trusts, the late Cole Porter. *The Biograph Girl* was Warner's first West End musical and it went on to play internationally. It introduced him to composer David Heneker, who was to become his mentor, and Mr Heneker and Warner were the subjects of the BBC Two documentary *The Making Of A Musical*. Warner wrote the new version of the classic Heneker/Cross musical *Half a Sixpence*.

Further work in London includes *Six for Gold*, a series of six one-act musicals performed over a two-night cycle, *Cinderella* at the London Palladium, *Tallulah for a Day*, starring Marti Webb, and *The Black and White Ball*, featuring the songs of Cole Porter and directed by Matthew White. For the UK national tour, Warner wrote *Son of a Preacher Man*, featuring the songs of Dusty Springfield, directed by Craig Revel Horwood. Warner's plays include *Laughing Dove*, *Wavelength* and *The Prospero Suite*, directed by John Doyle.

For BBC Worldwide, Warner wrote the arena show *Walking with Dinosaurs - The Arena Spectacular*, creating an entirely new genre of theatrical presentation. His work on this has won many international awards, including the Billboard Magazine Creative Content Award. Seen by over nine million people in more than 250 cities around the world, this twenty-million-dollar production is "the biggest family show of all time". An episode of *CSI: Las Vegas* was based upon the show and it has even been parodied on *The Simpsons*. Warner is part of the consortium including choreographer Arlene Phillips and musical director Mike Dixon for the internet-based project *Reality - The Musical*. He has worked extensively in Europe, with artists ranging from Sir Peter Ustinov to Al Jarreau. His musical *Garbo* received its world premiere at Oscarsteatern in Stockholm, Sweden, with music by Meat Loaf rock supremo Jim Steinman and Michael Reed. Warner has extensive writing credits for the BBC and was Script Associate of the BBC Classic Musicals Series, for which he adapted fourteen musicals and directed such international stars as Barbara Cook, Anthony Newley, Tyne Daly and Julia McKenzie. With Caroline Underwood, Warner is co-founder of The S&S Award, an international award for new musical theatre writing named in honour of his late parents. The Award has been presented, at its annual gala, by Michael Ball, Don Black, Nigel Harman and Janie Dee.

AUTHOR'S NOTE

The Biograph Girl is a work of my youth. I write things so differently these days that I had consigned it as a memory – though a very fond memory – to the back of my mind. In the years since its first production I have resisted all attempts to revive it, so what made me reconsider and believe again that it could have some relevance to the world today? Like many writers, I work a lot on instinct. When I first met the inspiring Jenny Eastop, Artistic Director of Mercurius Theatre, I sensed in a second that she had a "vision" for the show and that, through her vision, I might be made to realise how *The Biograph Girl* could be brought alive again for a modern-day audience. For a start, she wanted to reimagine the show for a different kind of space from its original West End incarnation and this, in turn, began to open my eyes to ways in which the show might live once more for a whole new panoply of different audiences. Amateur societies... youth groups... community ventures – each could tap into Jenny's vision and put their own stamp on this work of my juvenile past.

It helped, of course, that the different kind of space Jenny was talking about was London's Finborough Theatre. This venue, under the directorship of Neil McPherson, is world-renowned for its championship of new and challenging work. So if ever a place was likely to spark fresh thinking the Finborough was it. *The Biograph Girl* celebrates the early days of silent movies and what Jenny wanted to do was recapture the innocence of those pioneering times, its simplicity and its fun. In order to do this, she planned to strip the work right back. The original show had a cast of twelve with an orchestra of ten. Jenny's notion was to pare this down to a company of nine – with a single piano. Her thinking made me realise that the show might lend itself to any number of new approaches – after all, those early moviemakers experimented with anything that came to hand. An enterprising theatre group, for instance, might think of doing the show with actor-musicians. They would fit beautifully into this world of inspired improvisation.

In the same vein of thought, a show viewed through a microscope may also be seen through a magnifying glass. If you have people in your group who like to be onstage but draw the line at learning pages of dialogue, *The Biograph Girl* offers ample opportunity for crowd scenes, movie extras, protestors, cinema-goers and party people. Small is sublime and big is beautiful – whichever way you want to go!

Mercurius's new approach to the staging of the show has led me to go back to basics and re-examine the original material from scratch. I said earlier that the original production was a very fond memory and the main reason for this is that it introduced me to the co-writer who was to become my mentor. David Heneker was old enough to be my grandfather... we must have looked an odd writing couple... but we worked together from the start as a beauteous unit. Though David is no longer with us – correction: he and his influence is in my mind most every day of the week – I know what he wanted and would want from the show and I know the things we had to cut from the show at the time – but wish we hadn't. There are many reasons why material is cut from productions – time restraints; budget constrictions; mistaken judgements – and one of the things we most regretted was that we never really got to grips with the accusations of racism made against our central character D.W. Griffith. We did have a musical number addressing this called *Rivers of Blood*, which was lost on the road at Brighton. I'm thrilled to say that this number is now reinstated, together with a completely new song by David, *They Don't Call 'Em Flickers*. These, and some adjustments to dialogue scenes, are all a part of the new birth of our show

A new birth? Well... D.W. Griffith made a movie called *The Birth of a Nation* and it didn't do too badly. May the re-birth of *The Biograph Girl*, however you approach it, be an occasion for joy, enlightenment and maybe just a little Hollywood enchantment.

Warner Brown, 2018

ORIGINAL PRODUCTION NOTE

Our play covers sixteen crucial years in the history of the silent film. It starts in 1912 when Hollywood was created as the world's movie capital by an exodus of independent film-makers from New York. It ends in 1928, the year after Warner Brothers had made *The Jazz Singer* and silent movies were doomed. In the years between, films had been transformed into an art form, largely by the work of one man named David Wark Griffith. At the same time, they were made into the greatest entertainment force the world had ever seen and this was the work of a small group of businessmen, the movie moguls, of whom Adolph Zukor was the archetype. In between these extremes of art and business were the working artists, some of whom were born great, many of whom had greatness thrust upon them. Our play is dedicated to Lillian Gish, one who achieved greatness and was probably the best silent film actress of them all. We are indebted to her advice and her writings but she is not responsible for the historical inaccuracies which we have allowed in this dramatic impression, many of which she has pointed out to us. Although she and Mack Sennett both worked for D. W. Griffith, they never met. Griffith's fortunes did not decline immediately after *Intolerance* and he made three of his financially most successful films for United Artists. But we trust that overall we have given a valid impression of those creative years. This is our tribute to the pioneers and above all to Mr Griffith, whose film masterpieces can still stir an audience today.

Warner Brown and David Heneker

MUSIC USE NOTE

Licensees are solely responsible for obtaining formal written permission from copyright owners to use copyrighted music in the performance of this play and are strongly cautioned to do so. If no such permission is obtained by the licensee, then the licensee must use only original music that the licensee owns and controls. Licensees are solely responsible and liable for all music clearances and shall indemnify the copyright owners of the play(s) and their licensing agent, Samuel French, against any costs, expenses, losses and liabilities arising from the use of music by licensees. Please contact the appropriate music licensing authority in your territory for the rights to any incidental music.

USE OF COPYRIGHT MUSIC

A licence issued by Samuel French Ltd to perform this play does not include permission to use the incidental music specified in this copy. Where the place of performance is already licensed by the PERFORMING RIGHT SOCIETY (PRS) a return of the music used must be made to them. If the place of performance is not so licensed then application should be made to the PRS, 2 Pancras Square, London, N1C 4AG. (www.mcps-prs-alliance.co.uk). A separate and additional licence from PHONOGRAPHIC PERFORMANCE LTD, 1 Upper James Street, London W1F 9DE (www.ppluk.com) is needed whenever commercial recordings are used.

IMPORTANT BILLING AND CREDIT REQUIREMENTS

If you have obtained performance rights to this title, please refer to your licensing agreement for important billing and credit requirements.

THE BIOGRAPH GIRL

First presented at the Gardner Centre Theatre, University of Sussex, on 21 October, 1980. It was subsequently presented by Harold Fielding with the same cast at the Phoenix Theatre, London, on 19 November, 1980, when Miss Lillian Gish was in the audience.

Original Cast (in order of speaking)

LILLIAN	Kate Revill
DOROTHY	Sally Brelsford
MOMMA	Michelle Fine
MARY	Sheila White
GRIFFITH	Bruce Barry
EPPING	Richard Kates
ROSE	Jane Hardy
BITZER/ZUKOR	Ron Berglas
SENNETT	Guy Siner
PRESSMEN	Tano Rea, Philip Griffiths
USHERETTE	Helen Brindle

Directed by Victor Spinetti

Designed by John Pascoe

Musical direction and supervision by Michael Reed
Musical numbers staged by Irving Davies

The vocal score is published by Warner/Chappell Music Ltd, and is available from Samuel French Ltd, as are the bass, guitar and second piano parts

The original London cast album is available on Jay Records TER 1003 from Jay Records, 107 Kentish Town Road, London NW1 8PB.

CHARACTERS

LILLIAN GISH – a major star of silent films and a greatly respected figure of the American theatre to this day.

DOROTHY GISH – her younger sister and an equal success in silent films though in a lighter vein.

MRS MARY ROBINSON GISH – actress mother of Lillian and Dorothy. Her close friend was Mrs Charlotte Smith, mother of Gladys Smith.

GLADYS SMITH – achieved international fame and considerable fortune as Mary Pickford, "the world's sweetheart". Although not the original "Biograph Girl", she inherited the title when Florence Lawrence left Griffith to go to another studio.

DAVID WARK GRIFFITH – greatest of the pioneer film directors. His classic, *The Birth of a Nation,* is still frequently shown in specialist cinemas.

G. W. "BILLY" BITZER – Griffith's cameraman for sixteen years. Primitive cameras obliged him to improvise, which accidentally gave Griffith some of his finest effects, among them the fade-out.

JOHANNES CHARLEMAGNE EPPING – Griffith's accountant who secretly invested D.W.'s money in non-revocable annuities and saved him from spending his last years in penury.

ROSE SMITH – Griffith's long-time assistant, but the character as presented in this play is a compilation of several different people.

ADOLPH ZUKOR – one of the small-time salesmen (mostly from Central Europe) who became the big-time bosses of Hollywood. He died in 1976 aged 103.

MACK SENNETT – the king of silent film comedy who introduced Charlie Chaplin to the screen and created the Keystone Kops.

WALTER L. HALL – nicknamed "Spec" (short for perspective), pioneer scenic designer, largely responsible for the famous set design of Babylon. It was often thought Griffith produced his own designs on an ad hoc basis but Hall's plans exist to prove the contribution he made to *Intolerance.*

The musical may be performed with nine players. Various parts are doubled and tripled.

LILLIAN

DOROTHY

MOMMA

GRIFFITH

EPPING/ MAN OF THE SOUTH

ROSE

MARY

ZUKOR/BITZER

SENNETT

SPEC

NEWSBOY, PUBLICISTS, MOVIEGOERS

As many actors as possible should remain within the area of the stage throughout – in or out of their characters in the story – and should be involved as much as possible in passing props etc., to those who are performing and providing a general framework for the action. Permanent steps and cut-outs are moved by the actors themselves.

Repertory and amateur theatres may find it beneficial, by enlisting the co-operation of local film societies, to arrange screenings of appropriate silent films coinciding with their stage productions of *The Biograph Girl*.

The following films directed by D. W. Griffith are available for hire on 16mm from the British Film Institute Film & Video Library:

Judith of Bethulia (1914), with Lillian Gish (silent)
Birth of a Nation (1915), with Lillian Gish (sound)*
Intolerance (1916), with Lillian Gish (sound)*
Hearts of the World (1918), with Lillian and Dorothy Gish (and
  Noël Coward in a small role) (silent)
Broken Blossoms (1919), with Lillian Gish (silent)
True Heart Susie (1919), with Lillian Gish (silent)
Way Down East (1920), with Lillian Gish (sound)*
Orphans of the Storm (1922), with Lillian Gish (silent)
Sally of the Sawdust (1926) (sound)*
Abraham Lincoln (1929) (sound)

Rates for hire for single non-theatrical screenings, or for multiple non-theatrical and theatrical screenings, are available from the BFI, Belvedere Road, Lambeth, London SE1 8XT (020 7255 1444).

* Where "sound" is indicated, this means appropriate musical accompaniment has been added to the original silent film. *Abraham Lincoln* was made as "a talking picture".

MUSICAL NUMBERS

ACT I

1	Overture	
1(a)	Introduction to Act I	
2	The Moving Picture Show	Company
3	Workin' in Flickers	Mary
4	The Moment I Close My Eyes	Griffith
4(a)	Fight Music	
5	Diggin' Gold Dust	Company, Griffith and Mary
5(a)	Hearts and Flowers – Interlude	
6	Sennett's Mime	
7*	Every Lady	Lillian, Griffith and Bitzer
8*	I Just Wanted to Make Him Laugh	Sennett and Lillian
9	They Don't Call 'Em Flickers	Company
10	Rivers of Blood	Man of the South
10(a)	Workin' in Flickers – Reprise	
11	I Like to Be the Way I Am in My Own Front Parlour	Mary, Publicists and Pressmen
12	Beyond Babel	Griffith and Company

ACT II

13	A David Griffith Show	Company
14	More Than a Man	Lillian
14(a)	I Like to Be the Way I Am – Reprise	Mary
15	The Industry	Rose and Company
16	Gentle Fade	Griffith
17	One Long Party	Rose and Company
18	The Biograph Girl	Mary and Company
19	One of the Pioneers	Griffith
20	Put It in the Tissue Paper	Sennett, Mary and Lillian
21	Workin' in Flickers – Reprise	Company
22	Bows	
23	Tabs	

* Music for Nos. 7 and 8 by Warner Brown and David Heneker

ACT I

Permanent structures, right and left, suggest the wooden "towers" of an outdoor silent movie set. The area in between becomes many places during the course of the story, with a short flight of steps, centre, remaining throughout. All scenic effects are carried out within the idiom of early movie techniques and props, cut-outs and basic furniture are moved by the actors themselves.

MUSIC 1: "OVERTURE"

The set is furnished with outsize silent movies posters.

MUSIC 1(A): "INTRODUCTION TO ACT I"

The lights change to a faint, flickering blue, taking us in to a Nickleodeon circa 1912. Moviegoers, including **LILLIAN**, **DOROTHY** *and* **MOMMA GISH**, *bustle in to claim their "seats". They look out at the audience, as if watching a silent movie. Their faces register surprise, romance and fear.*

The lights revert to previous level.

MUSIC 2: "THE MOVING PICTURE SHOW"

Lines are taken individually at first, gradually developing into a **COMPANY** *number.*

ALL
    WE'VE SEEN BARNUM AND BAILEY OK THEY'RE OK

BOY
    AL KEECH ON UKELELE BOY HOW HE COULD PLAY

ALL
>THEY WERE GREAT ENTERTAINMENT ONLY YESTERDAY
>BUT NOW IT'S THE MOVING PICTURE SHOW

BOY
>TIME WAS I USED TO BE IN LINE FOR SEVERAL DAYS
>TO CATCH MILLIE DE LEON IN A PAIR OF STAYS

GIRL
>THAT WAS BACK WHEN BURLESQUE WAS STILL THE LATEST CRAZE

ALL
>BUT NOW IT'S THE MOVING PICTURE SHOW

GIRL
>SEE THAT COMICAL CHASE THERE
>BET SHE GETS ROMANCE
>FROM THAT FANCY-PANTS EARL

ANOTHER GIRL
>THEY'RE SPOONING

BOY
>SEE THAT BEAUTIFUL FACE THERE
>THAT'S HER PHOTOGRAPH
>THAT'S THE BIOGRAPH GIRL AIN'T SHE A PEARL

ANOTHER BOY
>I'M SWOONING

ALL
>ONCE WE THRILLED AT THE SIGHT OF EV'RY VAUDEVILLE
>WE THOUGHT TABLEAUS THE HEIGHT OF HISTRIONIC SKILL
>THEY'D GOT PLENTY OF ACTION GEE BUT THEY WERE STILL
>BUT NOW IT'S THE MOVING PICTURE
>NOW IT'S THE MOVING PICTURE
>NOW IT'S THE MOVING PICTURE SHOW

After the number, **LILLIAN**, **DOROTHY** *and* **MOMMA GISH** *remain.* **LILLIAN** *is the fragile beauty;* **DOROTHY** *the comedienne. They stare out front, incredulous.*

LILLIAN It was Gladys. Gladys Smith.

DOROTHY I couldn't believe it.

MOMMA Are you sure you're right? Our Gladys Smith?

DOROTHY You saw her, Momma – acting in the flickers.

MOMMA I don't want to worry you, Dorothy, but this place is a flea-pit.

LILLIAN Lots of girls do it now.

MOMMA But she couldn't. She's an actress. She wouldn't stoop to that.

DOROTHY Between stage jobs, Momma. Let's go see her.

MOMMA Let's go rescue her. But...we don't know where to go.

DOROTHY I do. I got the address from the man on the door.

MOMMA Perhaps she won't remember us.

LILLIAN She's not like that, Momma. Gladys won't forget her old friends.

DOROTHY Well, there's only one way to find out. Eleven East Fourteenth, that was it. American Mutoscope and Biograph Company, here we come!

They stare out one more time, incredulous still.

LILLIAN Gladys Smith – working in the flickers!

In unison they put their hands to their mouths.

DOROTHY, LILLIAN and **MOMMA** *exit.*

GLADYS SMITH (MARY) *appears at the top of the steps, in ringlets and frills.*

MUSIC 3: "WORKIN' IN FLICKERS"

MARY *(singing)*
WHAT I DO TO EARN A CENT
BUT SOMEONE'S GOTTA PAY THE RENT

I REALLY COULD DIE OF SHAME
WORKIN' IN FLICKERS
WHEN LIFE GETS THE LIMIT ME
I OPT FOR ANONYMITY
YOU GOTTA JUST CHANGE YOUR NAME
WORKIN' IN FLICKERS

WHEN I'M OUT OF A JOB
A VOICE FROM INSIDE ME
HOLLERS – GLADYS!
FORGET ABOUT ART YOU GOTTA GO GET SOME DOLLARS

THE THEATRE'S WHERE I'D RATHER BE
BUT MOMMA SHE DEPENDS ON ME
AN' BOY IT'S A PAYING GAME
WORKIN' IN FLICKERS

Dance (two stanzas i.e. 1st and 2nd eight).
WHEN I'M OUT OF A PLAY
THE NEIGHBOURHOOD THINKS I'M RESTING
BUT ME I'M ROUND AT THE BIOGRAPH STUDIO TESTING

SO WHEN I'M BROKE AND TIMES ARE BAD
IT'S HELLO FLICKERS
GOODBYE GLAD AS
OFF ROUND THE BLOCK I GO TO
CALL ON THE OLD BIO
HOPING THE WORLD DON'T KNOW
GLADYS SMITH HAS DESCENDED SO LOW
WORKIN' IN FLICKERS
WORKIN' IN FLICKERS

WORKIN' IN SH!
FLICKERS

MARY *exits.*

The lights rise on the Biograph Studio – but this is the rooftop of the building, as suggested by cut-out chimney pots and skylights. GRIFFITH, *a man of great presence and older than the others, is rehearsing a group of actors in front of* BITZER's *camera.* ROSE *is also onstage.* GRIFFITH *has just been interrupted by* EPPING, *the money-man.*

GRIFFITH You can't see, Epping. That's what's up with you and your money-men.

EPPING But Mr Griffith, you're overspent.

GRIFFITH Never be cheap, Epping.

EPPING But...

GRIFFITH Think cheap, and what do you get?

ROSE
BITZER } *(together)* { Cheap thoughts!
ACTORS

GRIFFITH Now...I need a girl for the scene. Where's a girl? I asked you to get me a girl.

ROSE Mr Griffith, I know you're a genius, but...

GRIFFITH No, my dear, not a genius. There are many directors... some directors...a few directors who can make moving pictures just as good as I can. But do they stick at it? No they do not. Only I am prepared to carry on. Relentlessly. Endlessly learning. Because it's what we have to do. None of us knows about pictures. Me – what do I know? But by working...by working we shall learn.

EPPING Mr Griffith, they told me to tell you they pay for the whole of the actor and the whole of the actor's what they want to see.

GRIFFITH Put the camera up close to her, Epping, and you get her face. Her face is more important than her feet.

EPPING But...no disrespect to Mr Bitzer, I'm sure, but...they told me to tell you the background's fuzzy.

GRIFFITH *takes hold of* EPPING.

GRIFFITH Look at me, Epping. Can you see all of me? No you can not. You can see half of me – right? Now that chimney pot in back of me...well? ...Is it or is it not fuzzy?

EPPING Fuzzy.

GRIFFITH *(releasing him)* Good God, Epping, what I showed them on that screen is what they see a thousand times a day. And they don't even know it.

EPPING I don't understand you, Mr Griffith. And I speak for all of us too. You know so much and...

GRIFFITH I've told you – I know scarcely anything at all. Just what's in here. *(He points to his head)* And what's in here. *(He points to his heart)*

EPPING But we can't *see* in there, Mr Griffith.

GRIFFITH I can. And it's all I need to make the world stand still.

MUSIC 4: "THE MOMENT I CLOSE MY EYES"

Singing.
I'VE ONLY TO CLOSE MY EYES
AND I'M AWAY ON THE WING
I'M IN A WORLD WHERE I'M KING
THE MOMENT I CLOSE MY EYES

AT ONCE I CAN SEE A FACE
A GLANCE A SMILE OR A TEAR
IS THAT A HEARTBEAT I HEAR?
THE MOMENT I SEE THAT FACE

ALL THE PICTURES IN MY MIND I SEE QUITE CLEARLY
BUT ARE THEY REALLY THE ONES I NEED?
ALL THE SAME I MUST ADMIT THEY HAVE THEIR USES
IF THEIR EXCUSE IS
THEY PLANT A SEED

AND SO AS I CLOSE MY EYES
I'M LIVING LIFE IN THE ROUND

AN IMAGE LOST HAS BEEN FOUND
THE MOMENT I CLOSE MY EYES

BITZER *(spoken quietly; at* **GRIFFITH***'s side)* Mr Griffith, will you look at this lens?

GRIFFITH *(raising his hand)*
TIME TO THINK TIME TO PLAN
TIME FOR CONTEMPLATION
THESE ARE THINGS EVERY MAN
NEEDS FOR CONCENTRATION
IF HE'S IN THE BUSINESS OF CREATION

I'VE ONLY TO CLOSE MY EYES
AND I'M AWAY ON THE WING
I'M IN A WORLD WHERE I'M KING
THE MOMENT I CLOSE MY EYES

AT ONCE I CAN SEE A FACE
A GLANCE A SMILE OR A TEAR
IS THAT A HEARTBEAT I HEAR?
THE MOMENT I SEE THAT FACE

ALL THE PICTURES IN MY MIND I SEE QUITE CLEARLY
BUT ARE THEY REALLY THE ONES I NEED?
ALL THE SAME I MUST ADMIT THEY HAVE THEIR USES
IF THEIR EXCUSE IS
THEY PLANT A SEED

THE ONE THING I REALISE
WHEN LIFE AND I DISAGREE
IT'S NOW AS CLEAR AS CAN BE
THE MOMENT I CLOSE MY EYES I CAN SEE

(speaking) Now, Billy, about that lens...

GRIFFITH *exits with* **BITZER***.*

LILLIAN, **MOMMA** *and* **DOROTHY** *enter from the other side.*

MOMMA What've we come on the roof for? Has he got her in a loft?

DOROTHY Quiet, Momma. This is where they said she is.

LILLIAN *(to* ROSE*)* Excuse me. We've come to see Gladys Smith.

ROSE No one here by that name.

DOROTHY But we saw her. In one of your pictures.

ROSE What picture?

DOROTHY It was... Oh – do they have names?

LILLIAN Of course they have names. It was...well, it had a lot of geese in it.

ROSE *Lena and the Geese*! You'll be meaning Little Mary.

MOMMA Mary?

ROSE Why didn't you say so in the first place? You'll be meaning Mary Pickford – the Biograph Girl.

They all stare at her.

She's here.

MOMMA On the roof?

ROSE *(laughing)* It's where we make the movies. Out in God's sunlight.

GRIFFITH *returns with* BITZER, *who is carrying a different kind of lens.*

Excuse me now, I've got to go and help Mr Griffith.

LILLIAN So *that's* Griffith, is it?

ROSE You can't speak to...

LILLIAN Mr Griffith, you've got our friend and we want her back.

GRIFFITH *(turning to* LILLIAN*)* Well...have I now?

ROSE I'm sorry, Mr Griffith, I tried to...

GRIFFITH Have no worries, Rose. The young lady has obviously cast me as a White Slaver. It is up to me to show her that I'm cast against type.

LILLIAN We want to see Gladys. Our friend, Gladys Smith.

GRIFFITH Then you shall see her, my dear. Or rather – you shan't.

MOMMA There! She's being kept against her will.

GRIFFITH Gladys Smith is no more, madam.

MOMMA *(aghast)* Dead?

GRIFFITH Transmogrified. *(He looks off)* You want to view the body?

They nod their heads.

Then, ladies, stand aside.

The ladies stand aside.

MARY *runs on with a sack of letters. She does not see the* **GISHES**.

MARY Mr Griffith, look at all these letters.

GRIFFITH I never read letters, Mary.

MARY They're not addressed to you. They're for me.

GRIFFITH They're for the Biograph Girl.

MARY That *is* me.

GRIFFITH Then you should be very happy.

MARY *(stamping her foot)* Well I'm *not* happy. Why should I be known as the Biograph Girl when all the other stars in all the other companies get called by their own names?

GRIFFITH I don't believe in the star system, Mary.

MARY All the same – these letters should be addressed to Mary Pickford. What's the point in changing your name if it never gets used? *(Suddenly she spots the* **GISHES**. *Her manner changes instantly)* Lillian! Dorothy...!

MARY *rushes over to them. They all hug.*

LILLIAN I told you, Momma. I told you it was Gladys Smith.

MARY ...And Mrs Gish. Why, it's lovely to see you. After all this time.

MOMMA How's your mother, dear?

MARY Fine. We're...

DOROTHY We saw you in a picture. *Lena and the Geese.*

MOMMA Oh, what are you doing in the pictures, Gladys? Are things *that* bad?

MARY *(laughing)* No, no. You've got it all wrong. I've been making movies for three years now and the family's been together all this time. I'm earning more than I've ever done before – much more.

MOMMA But your name. When we asked for you they said you changed it to...

DOROTHY Mary Pickford, Momma.

MOMMA Exactly. What is it, Gladys – shame?

There is a pause.

MARY Yes. *(changing her tone)* No. I *was* ashamed...till I saw how much money I could make. And that made it different. That put it in a new category altogether.

LILLIAN But you're legitimate, Gladys. From the theatre, like us.

DOROTHY Oh, how did you do it? How did you get in to pictures?

LILLIAN Don't worry, dear. Your secret's safe with us.

MARY It's no secret – I made a test.

MOMMA A test?

MARY For Mr Griffith. He's a genius, you know. *(She lowers her voice)* You wouldn't believe it, but I've been offered twice as much from another company already. We're living in a lovely apartment and Momma's got an automobile.

DOROTHY An automobile!

MARY You know, you should try the flickers.

MOMMA*'s face turns to stone.*

At least while you're looking for a play.

MOMMA It's out of the question, girls.

GRIFFITH *(clapping his hands)* OK, back to work. You, young Mary, get ready for your next scene.

MARY Yes, Mr Griffith. *(to the* GISHES*)* Byee, don't go away now.

GRIFFITH *(to* ROSE*)* And you, young lady...

MARY *(returning to* LILLIAN*)* I can't believe it, seeing you again.

GRIFFITH ...find me a girl.

MARY *exits.*

ROSE Mr Griffith, you haven't given me enough time.

GRIFFITH But I will make of her a vision.

ROSE Vision or not, Mr Griffith, young ladies don't want to come here.

MOMMA I told you, Dorothy.

ROSE Because of the combine.

MOMMA Combine?

ROSE Big business. The guys who own the patents.

MOMMA I don't know about patents.

ROSE Cameras and equipment and film. They buy up patents to all the different stuff so they can force individual operators out of the movie game.

MOMMA But why should this effect the young girls?

ROSE Because of the raids.

DOROTHY Raids?

ROSE They send their men to shoot up our cameras.

MOMMA They don't sound nice men to me.

ROSE They're hoodlums. Riff-raff off the streets.

MOMMA And have they...raided you today yet?

ROSE Not so far. We've been saying our prayers.

GRIFFITH OK – hold it!

> **GRIFFITH** *looks nonplussed, then he turns and spots* **LILLIAN**.

I'll take you.

LILLIAN Who – me?

GRIFFITH Quickly. I haven't got all day.

LILLIAN I...I don't even know what you're talking about.

GRIFFITH I'm talking about reality. Truth. I'm talking about the movies.

LILLIAN It's not my idea of the movies.

GRIFFITH *(leading her in camera range)* And what *is* your idea, Miss...?

LILLIAN Gish. Lillian Gish. I don't know, I'm not an expert.

GRIFFITH There are no experts. We're in at the birth, Miss Gish. The start of the revolution.

LILLIAN There you are – that's it. You see a revolution. I see pictures of actors on a screen. Moving pictures. Out-of-work actors.

GRIFFITH And don't those pictures do anything to you?

LILLIAN They make me think "How clever".

GRIFFITH Like a phonograph?

LILLIAN A scientific marvel...yes.

GRIFFITH No!

LILLIAN I...?

GRIFFITH Don't they make you laugh, don't they make you cry?

LILLIAN Sometimes they do, but...

GRIFFITH Don't they move your spirit, don't they tug at your soul?

LILLIAN I'm from the theatre, Mr Griffith. Frankly, no they do not.

GRIFFITH Then come on the journey with me.

LILLIAN Journey? What journey?

GRIFFITH The journey of discovery.

LILLIAN I can't go without my mother, Mr Griffith.

GRIFFITH No, Miss Gish. I didn't think you could.

LILLIAN Can you tell me – is it far?

GRIFFITH As far as we like to make it.

LILLIAN And will we know when we've got there?

GRIFFITH Yes, Miss Gish. Somehow I think we will.

There is a change of light.

MUSIC 4(A): "FIGHT MUSIC"

The rooftop is invaded by a gang of hoods who attempt to shoot up the mutograph camera.

A fight ensues as **GRIFFITH** *and his* **MEN** *attempt to ward off the baddies. Out of the turmoil we hear* **MOMMA***'s voice.*

MOMMA Which side's the law on?

ROSE *(wielding a prop chair)* Technically – theirs.

MOMMA So Mr Griffith's cheating, then?

ROSE Do you believe in morals, Mrs Gish?

MOMMA I should say I do!

ROSE Then stick up for Griffith! You'll be on the goodies' side!

MOMMA Go get 'em, girls!

The ladies, brandishing pocket books, chase the hoods off the set. They return to **GRIFFITH**, *who has sustained a bloody nose.*

GRIFFITH Rose!

ROSE Yes, Mr Griffith?

GRIFFITH Bring me a map, Rose.

ROSE Where of, Mr Griffith?

GRIFFITH Anywhere. So long as it's a heck of ways from here.

ROSE California do you, Mr Griffith?

GRIFFITH California will do me nicely.

ROSE *produces a map.* **GRIFFITH** *takes it.*

Your thumb, Rose.

ROSE *holds out her thumb.* **GRIFFITH** *takes it and, with a magnificent flourish, presses it down at a spot on the map he has chosen at random.*

Well, Rose?

ROSE *(looking at the map)* It says "Edendale", Mr Griffith.

GRIFFITH Then that's where we shall go, my dear. Where we shall go to get away.

ROSE Edendale, Mr Griffith?

GRIFFITH *looks down at the thumb and turns it slightly, to reveal for himself the obscured place name.*

GRIFFITH Edendale...and Hollywood.

ACT I 15

MUSIC 5: "DIGGIN' GOLD DUST"

During this, a "Griffith Wipe" is effected on the cyclorama to take us from the gloom of New York City to the golden sunlight of California.

The **COMPANY** *flood on;* **GRIFFITH** *and the* **GISHES** *have gone.* **MARY** *enters in a yellow gingham dress.*

MARY California? Isn't that where them prospectors went?

COMPANY *(singing)*
DIGGIN' GOLD DUST ONLY JUST BEGUN
DIGGIN' GOLD DUST DOLLARS TO BE WON
JOIN THE GOLD RUSH
EVERY MOTHER'S SON AND DAUGHTER
DOING WHAT THEY DIDN'T OUGHT TO DO
SO WHY DON'T YOU DO IT TOO?
DIGGIN' GOLD DUST JOIN THE BROTHERHOOD
DIGGIN' GOLD DUST MARY DOES IT GOOD
NOW SHE'S GOT A BANK ACCOUNT THAT'S QUICKLY GROWING
BOY, IS SHE INTENT ON GOING FAR
TO BE A STAR
BE A STAR

IF YOU WANT GREENBACKS IN YOUR POUCH
YOU CAN'T AFFORD TO BE A SLOUCH
WHO KNOWS IT MAY BE TRUE
YOU'LL COME THROUGH
ON THE CASTING COUCH

SEE THAT GOLD DUST GLITTER IN THE PAN
WATCH IT SETTLE
BOY, THAT METAL
HAS MORE VALUE THAN
HALF A TON O' DIAMONDS
AND A COAT OF ASTRAKHAN

DIGGIN' GOLD DUST ONLY JUST BEGUN
DIGGIN' GOLD DUST DOLLARS TO BE WON

JOIN THE GOLD RUSH
EVERY MOTHER'S SON AND DAUGHTER
DOING WHAT THEY DIDN'T OUGHT TO DO
SO WHY DON'T YOU
SO WHY DON'T YOU
SO WHY DON'T YOU AND YOU AND YOU AND YOU
DO IT TOO DO IT TOO DO IT TOO DO IT TOO YEAH
DO IT TOO DO IT TOO DO IT TOO DO IT TOO?
YOU CAN DO IT TOO

The COMPANY *has now cleared, leaving* MARY *alone.*

MARY *(waiting at an imaginary door)* I'm waiting for Mr Zukor. He's the boss of Paramount Pictures.

Two MINIONS *enter, carrying* ZUKOR's *chair and the circle of Paramount stars.*

They set the chair at the top of the steps and fix the circle of stars to it so that it frames ZUKOR's *head when he sits.*

ZUKOR *enters. He is the typical movie magnate with the cunning of a benign fox. He sits on his chair.*

In this scene MARY *is very, very sweet.*

ZUKOR Miss Pickford, I've been speaking to your mother.

MARY Yes, Mr Zukor.

ZUKOR She's a very...determined lady, Miss Pickford.

MARY She only wants what's best for me, Mr Zukor.

ZUKOR Don't we all, my dear?

MARY She only wants to see that if I leave Mr Griffith...and I emphasize the "if", Mr Zukor...I leave for something worthwhile.

ZUKOR Apparently her idea of worthwhile is five hundred dollars a week.

MARY *smiles like a little girl.*

MUSIC 5(A): "HEARTS AND FLOWERS – INTERLUDE"

MARY Oh Mr Zukor...it's always been a silly, childish little ambition of mine, you know. I said to myself when I was five years old... I did... "Mary" I said – or Gladys, as I was known in those days" Gladys...before you're twenty, girl, you must be on five hundred a week. For the sake of the family." And I'm nineteen now, Mr Zukor. Nineteen and quite a big bit.

ZUKOR But playing twelve, my dear.

MARY So much extra effort.

There is a pause.

ZUKOR Mary – there's something I'd like you to see. *(He comes down the steps)*

MARY I think perhaps we should finish our conversation first. Momma would prefer it that way, I'm sure.

ZUKOR It's only over the street, my dear. Just through the window. *(He points out front)*

MARY *(very sweetly)* Momma says I'm going to be the world's sweetheart, you see. And the world's sweetheart is worth five hundred dollars of anybody's money.

ZUKOR Three dollars a day. Less than four years ago you were on three dollars a day.

MARY Five, Mr Zukor. Momma always saw to it that I got a little more than the others.

ZUKOR A very determined lady, Mary.

MARY Oh, we're agreed on that.

ZUKOR Come to the window. There's a good child.

MARY *joins him. They both look out front.*

MARY Oh, Mr Zukor – look what you gone and done. Electric lights! My name in electric lights!

ZUKOR Read it, Mary. Read it out loud.

MARY *(hesitantly, for she has had little education)* "Mary Pickford. America's Sweetheart" ...And there I was talking money. *(She pauses)* If it was only for myself, of course, I wouldn't mind. But there's my sister to consider and my little brother too...

ZUKOR You're on three hundred with Griffith.

MARY And I really think Momma should have a little good-will cash. For being such an inspiration.

ZUKOR She's a figure in mind, no doubt.

MARY Mr Zukor, you're the boss of Paramount Pictures. There's not a thing in the world you cannot do. *(She pauses)* I'm so *awful* at money-talk. But then, I'm only a child.

ZUKOR Nineteen and quite a big bit, my dear.

MARY But playing twelve.

ZUKOR *(musing)* "America's Sweetheart" ...OK, you win. I'll have the contract drawn up.

MARY *(producing a contract)* Oh, Mr Zukor, Momma's done that already! To save you the bother, you know.

ZUKOR Five hundred dollars and you not twenty. My dear, will you be able to manage?

MARY No more nickel bus rides. No more lousy one-night stands. If we can manage one-night stands, Mr Zukor, we can manage five hundred dollars.

ZUKOR Yes. Yes, somehow I think you can. *(He turns to go)*

MARY Mr Zukor?

ZUKOR My dear?

MARY *(with a nod towards the "window")* Thank you. For that. I'll try to be worth it.

ACT I

ZUKOR Just try to be worth the five hundred dollars. The rest'll take care of itself.

ZUKOR *and* MARY *exit together.*

Simultaneously GRIFFITH *sweeps on with the* COMPANY, SENNETT *is there too, lurking in the background.*

GRIFFITH ...If you're on location, Epping, you can't afford to be cheap. Pay the cop who keeps order for you. Tip the guy whose front yard you use. Slip a buck to the kid who brings the lunches. Keep them happy, Epping.

EPPING But two hundred dollars, Mr Griffith!

GRIFFITH When I go back I'll be two hundred times as welcome.

EPPING Look, I know you're a genius...

GRIFFITH I am not a genius, but I tell you this. We are playing now to a new audience. What we film today will stir the hearts of the world tomorrow. For they will understand what we're saying. From Moscow to Paris, from Peking to Arkansas – we can reach them all. The whole world, Epping – go tell 'em that.

EPPING The whole world?

EPPING *exits.*

SENNETT *comes forward.*

SENNETT Can I do my test now, Mr Griffith?

GRIFFITH Test?

SENNETT You promised me. Today you said. You promised me today.

GRIFFITH All right, Mr...?

SENNETT Sennett. Mack Sennett.

GRIFFITH All right, Mr Sennett...what can you show me?

SENNETT I can't show you anything, Mr Griffith. It's all in my head.

GRIFFITH It's no use to me in there, my good man. Come back when you can give me Shakespeare and Racine and drama and truth.

SENNETT Truth...truth... I can give you *my* truth, Mr Griffith.

GRIFFITH Very well, sir. Fire my imagination.

SENNETT Fire? ...Fire! ...A fireman!

MUSIC 6: "SENNETT'S MIME"

Refer to the piano score for lettered music cues.

SENNETT *pretends to go to sleep. Snore! Snore!*

A   Bell sounds. He wakes up – dresses – slides down the pole

B   (Swanee whistle)

C   Fire engine – leaves without him – he runs after it and...

D   ...falls (tom-tom)

E   He looks up and sees the fire on the top storey of a high building

F   Positioning ladder

G   Climbs ladder

H   He looks down – gets dizzy

I   Continues climbing

J   Waves smoke away

K   He looks at the window and sees a girl

L   He looks down

M   He puts the girl on his shoulder...

N   ...and slides down the ladder

O   He kisses the girl (duck quack)

P   He sees that she is not quite as pretty as he thought and drops her...

Q   ...and steps on her (klaxon or B-drum)

R   Mimes throwing a custard pie at Griffith (swanee whistle up)

S   Griffith mimes throwing one back... (swanee whistle down)

T   Pie in face

U   Wipes it off

GRIFFITH What I need is truth. What I need is another actor.

SENNETT *is "hooked off", vaudeville-style.*

There is a blackout.

The lights come up.

BITZER, *with his camera, and* **LILLIAN** *enter.*

There is a great deal of "on-set" activity in the background.

BITZER D.W.... D.W., this young girl says you want her shot in to the sun.

GRIFFITH And she tells you right, Billy.

BITZER But if I do that she'll come out black on the screen. She'll have a coal-black face.

GRIFFITH Ever looked at a sunrise, Billy? Radiance – that's what you see if you look at a sunrise. Radiance and long black shadows and...

BITZER Coal-black faces, Mr Griffith.

GRIFFITH She'll have a halo over her head, Billy. We'll give it a try tomorrow.

GRIFFITH *takes* LILLIAN *by the hand as* BITZER *goes to adjust the camera.*

I've had a dream, Miss Lillian.

LILLIAN Pleasant, I hope, Mr Griffith?

GRIFFITH No. Revolutionary.

LILLIAN About the flickers?

GRIFFITH Flickers! I never want to hear that word again.

LILLIAN I'm sorry, I thought...

GRIFFITH You thought what everybody thinks. That pictures are a novelty in a nickelodeon. Well, maybe that's all they are just at the moment, but then...I'm the only one who's had the dream. *(He goes to her)* Do you know what pictures are, Miss Lillian? Drawings or postal cards or any kind of picture?

LILLIAN Pictures are...pictures.

GRIFFITH Pictures are glimpses of a man's soul.

LILLIAN *laughs, but* GRIFFITH *is serious.*

You laugh at your flickers, Miss Gish. But you wouldn't laugh at the *Mona Lisa*.

LILLIAN The *Mona Lisa*'s art.

GRIFFITH My pictures are a new kind of art. Maybe more important.

LILLIAN Really, I...

GRIFFITH That's putting it mildly. I tell you, I'm on to something. Something more real than...

LILLIAN No.

GRIFFITH What?

LILLIAN Dreams aren't real. That's why they're dreams.

GRIFFITH You don't see what I'm talking about.

ACT I

LILLIAN You're talking about life as it's dreamt. I was referring to life as it is. *(She pauses)* Life as it's dreamt belongs to the theatre, Mr Griffith.

GRIFFITH Can the theatre show me inside somebody's mind?

LILLIAN Only God can do that.

GRIFFITH No – maybe I can too. I film you in close-up. You are thinking of your long-lost brother over the seas. I film him in close-up. Then I cut in to my picture of you with a picture of him. You smile...in that deceptively innocent way of yours...and there we have it. Thought and reaction to thought.

LILLIAN I barely understand what a close-up is, Mr Griffith.

GRIFFITH *(scoffing)* The theatre!

LILLIAN Mr Griffith...

GRIFFITH Can the theatre capture your soul, Miss Lillian, and beam it round the world? *(He leads* **LILLIAN** *in camera range)* I'm going to make a picture.

LILLIAN Of course you are, Mr Griffith.

GRIFFITH No – not just any picture. A very special picture. *(He pauses)* I'm going to tell the story of the birth of America.

LILLIAN Oh.

GRIFFITH Is that all you can say? Oh?

LILLIAN I...

GRIFFITH My Poppa told me stories, Miss Lillian. Stories of the earth. Of the South. I'm going to fight now to tell these stories, to tell the truth. And I want you to help me.

LILLIAN Mr Griffith, all I can say is – I'll do my best.

> **LILLIAN** *looks at* **GRIFFITH**. *The activity of the scene around her suddenly fades.*
>
> *MUSIC 7: "EVERY LADY"*

Singing.
EVERY LADY
NEEDS A MASTER
WHO CAN GUIDE HER THROUGH
I'M NO EXCEPTION
I NEED A MASTER TOO

IN MY WORLD THERE'S
ONLY ONE MAN
WHO WILL EVER DO
I'D BE OBLIGED IF
MY MASTER COULD BE YOU

GIVEN A GIRL WHO'S INGÉNUE
GIVEN A MAN WHO'S STRONG
SUCH AN OLD-FASHIONED RESPECT IS DUE
HOW CAN IT BE SEEN AS WRONG?

THERE IS COMMANDMENT IN YOUR EYES
ANYONE WHO LOOKS CAN SEE
MAYBE YOU'LL CUT ME DOWN TO SIZE
IF I SAY IT'S JUST FOR ME

EVERY LADY
NEEDS A MASTER
WHO CAN GUIDE HER THROUGH
I'M NO EXCEPTION
I NEED A MASTER TOO

The music continues. Time is frozen.

GRIFFITH *(speaking)* Billy...Billy, look. I can do it with her. This is the one.

BITZER *(speaking)* The one, D.W.?

GRIFFITH *(speaking)* Yes, Billy. The Griffith Heroine.

BITZER *(speaking)* But...

GRIFFITH *(singing)*
HERE SHE IS
MY OWN CREATION
BILLY – CAN'T YOU SEE?

ONE LITTLE GIRL WILL
CONQUER THE WORLD FOR ME

SEE ME SHAPE HER
TILL AT LAST SHE'S
HOW SHE'S GOT TO BE
STANDING FOR LOVE
FOR LIFE AND FOR PURITY

BITZER (*looking at* **LILLIAN** *through the camera; singing*)
TIME AND AGAIN HE HAS HIS SCHEMES
SOME BARELY LAST THE DAY
IS THIS THE GIRL WHO HAUNTS HIS DREAMS?
I'M NOT THE MAN TO SAY

WHAT ARE THE POINTS TO EMPHASIZE?
THAT'S ALL I NEED TO KNOW
LOOK AT THE GIRL YOU SEE HER EYES
THAT'S WHAT HE WANTS TO SHOW

Duet.

LILLIAN	**GRIFFITH**
EVERY LADY	IN MY GRASP
NEEDS A MASTER	MY OWN CREATION
WHO CAN GUIDE HER THROUGH	(*speaking*) Billy – can't you see?
I'M NO EXCEPTION	(*singing*) ONE LITTLE GIRL WILL
I NEED A MASTER TOO	CONQUER THE WORLD FOR ME
IN MY WORLD THERE'S	SEE ME SHAPE HER
ONLY ONE MAN	TILL AT LAST SHE'S
WHO WILL EVER DO	HOW SHE'S GOT TO BE
I'D BE OBLIGED IF	STANDING FOR LOVE
MY MASTER COULD BE YOU	FOR LIFE AND FOR PURITY

As they finish singing, we are aware of **GRIFFITH** *very close by* **LILLIAN**'s *side.*

GRIFFITH Lillian! Miss Lillian, where's that look you had in your eyes? What was in your mind then? I want to film that look.

LILLIAN I...

GRIFFITH You're wandering.

LILLIAN I'm sorry.

GRIFFITH We're about the here and now.

LILLIAN I'm sorry. I... I'll try and get it again.

GRIFFITH We're about something that's real, Miss Lillian. Like we've never known before.

LILLIAN I'm sorry. I've said I'm sorry.

GRIFFITH I don't want you to be sorry, Miss Lillian. I want you to be real.

GRIFFITH *strides off the set followed by* BITZER, *who leaves his camera behind.*

LILLIAN *is at a loss as to what to do.*

SENNETT *enters, crossing the set to* LILLIAN.

SENNETT Pardon me, but could you direct me to the door marked "Exit"?

LILLIAN There isn't one. We're outside.

SENNETT I was speaking figuratively.

LILLIAN There isn't one figuratively either. You just keep going till you hit the street.

SENNETT *(turning away)* Could you tell me where I could get a cup of coffee?

LILLIAN Figurative or real?

SENNETT It doesn't really matter. *(He turns to go)*

LILLIAN If you'd like hot tea I have some in my bag.

ACT I

SENNETT Tea?

LILLIAN In a thermos. Oatmeal cookies too.

SENNETT Thanks all the same, but I don't think oatmeal cookies'd help very much.

LILLIAN That bad, is it?

SENNETT Worse. I did a test for Mr Griffith.

LILLIAN Negative?

   SENNETT *nods his head.*

   Sure?

SENNETT Positive.

LILLIAN Oh.

SENNETT That's what I thought.

LILLIAN Did he... did he tell you what was wrong?

SENNETT Everything.

LILLIAN I see.

SENNETT Not enough reality. Not enough truth.

LILLIAN Oh, is *that* all?

SENNETT Isn't it enough?

LILLIAN No... No one ever has enough truth for Mr Griffith. The man isn't born who's real enough for him.

   They sigh together.

SENNETT I only wanted one thing anyway.

LILLIAN One thing? What was that?

SENNETT I wanted... Oh, never mind.

   SENNETT *is shy, but* LILLIAN *perseveres.*

LILLIAN I'm Lillian Gish and I wish you'd tell me what you wanted from Mr Griffith.

SENNETT Oh, I didn't want anything *from* him. I wanted to do something *to* him – it's a different thing altogether.

LILLIAN And what did you want to do to him, Mr...?

SENNETT *(offering his hand)* Sennett. Mack Sennett's the name. I'm from theatre.

LILLIAN *(shaking hands)* You too?

SENNETT You mean...?

LILLIAN Legit.

SENNETT Vaudeville.

LILLIAN So you wanted to...?

SENNETT Exactly.

LILLIAN I see the problem. You're a comedy man.

SENNETT Right!

MUSIC 8: "I JUST WANTED TO MAKE HIM LAUGH"

Singing.

FIRST I GIVE HIM THE WARMING-UP ROUTINE
I JUST WANTED TO MAKE HIM LAUGH
HE KEP' TRYING TO MAKE ME ACT RACINE
WHILE I KEP' TRYING TO MAKE HIM LAUGH

DO MY COMEDY GAGS FROM A TO ZEE
I'M STILL TRYING TO RAISE A SMILE
HE SAYS GIVE ME "TO BE OR NOT TO BE"
WHEN HE SHOULD'VE BEEN ROLLING IN THE AISLE

I'M NOT AT ALL A STRAIGHT DRAMATIC ACTOR
I COULDN'T PLAY THE HERO IN *EAST LYNNE*
I DON'T WANT ANY LAURELS FOR PLAYS THAT DEAL IN MORALS
I JUST WANT TO SEE A MILLION-DOLLAR GRIN

MAYBE GIVEN ANOTHER TIME AND PLACE
HE'D HAVE TAKEN ME ON HIS STAFF
IF I HADN'T WANTED TO MAKE HIM...

ACT I

LILLIAN *(singing)*
...LAUGH

There is a dance routine over the first two bars – instrumental – until.

SENNETT *(singing)*
I JUST WANTED TO MAKE HIM LAUGH.

A further dance routine over the fifth and sixth bars – instrumental– until.

LILLIAN *(singing)* ⎫
⎬ *(together)* ⎰ YOU JUST WANTED TO
SENNETT *(speaking)* ⎭ ⎱ MAKE HIM LAUGH
Who's Racine?

Dance.

LILLIAN *(speaking)* Hey, you're something else.

Dance.

LILLIAN *(speaking)* You're an actor.

SENNETT *(speaking)* I guess I am. But a comedy actor.

(singing)
I'M JUST GETTING THE BIG PAY-OFF LINED UP
WHEN HE SLICES THE INTERVIEW IN HALF

LILLIAN AND YOU JUST WANTED TO MAKE HIM LAUGH

SENNETT I JUST WANTED TO MAKE HIM LAUGH

LILLIAN ⎫ ⎰ YOU JUST WANTED TO MAKE HIM LAUGH
SENNETT ⎭ *(together)* ⎱ I JUST WANTED TO MAKE HIM LAUGH

At the end of the number **ROSE** *enters with a clipboard.*

ROSE Mr Sennett, my name's Rose Smith. I'm a cutter for Griffith.

SENNETT Cutter? Does that come under the wardrobe department?

ROSE *(laughing)* No, it means I splice for him. His films. He's sent me with a message for you.

SENNETT For me? You must be mistaken.

ROSE No, no – he says – *(She reads from her clipboard)* he says you're real. Says you've got truth.

SENNETT But...?

ROSE *(looking up)* Not as an actor, you understand.

SENNETT Then...?

ROSE As a writer. He's offering you a job.

SENNETT Mack Sennett Bylines?

ROSE Twenty-five dollars a week. *(aside, to LILLIAN)* Mary gets five hundred.

LILLIAN That's with Zukor. *(She extends her hand)* Congratulations, Mr Sennett. I can't tell you how...

But SENNETT *has become rigid with shock.* ROSE *and* LILLIAN *look at him happily, then* ROSE *clicks her fingers and two stagehands come forward.*

The stagehands carry SENNETT *off, still in his upright position.*

ROSE *then follows off as* GRIFFITH *enters from the opposite direction with* EPPING *and* BITZER.

The set is full of activity again.

GRIFFITH Miss Lillian!

LILLIAN Mr Griffith... I thought you'd finished for the day.

GRIFFITH Finished? I've only just begun.

EPPING Mr Griffith... Mr Griffith, may I speak? For a moment, please.

GRIFFITH *(his attention now on LILLIAN)* Feel free, Mr Epping. My ear is yours.

ACT I

EPPING *(with a glance at* LILLIAN*)* Perhaps...

GRIFFITH Don't worry about Miss Gish, Mr Epping. She is the soul of discretion.

EPPING I've been telling Bitzer. Now I think you ought to know. Come Thursday there'll be no cheques for your company.

There is a pause, then GRIFFITH *gives a nervous laugh.*

GRIFFITH *(to* LILLIAN*)* Then let's get to work straight away. If we don't get your scene today there's no money to make it tomorrow.

EPPING Mr Griffith – you've spent already fifty thousand dollars. You had five hundred costumes made at least... He's even hired a philharmonic orchestra.

GRIFFITH Best band west of the Mississippi!

EPPING *(frantically)* Mr Griffith...

GRIFFITH *(holding up a hand)* Epping, I shall be frugal. See this. *(He holds up his right foot to reveal a hole in the sole of his shoe)* Well, I'm not going to buy new shoes until we start getting money back at the box office. That's a deal for you, sir!

EPPING But...

GRIFFITH A deal, Mr Epping.

There is a pause. BITZER *wanders away.*

EPPING I'll do what I can, Mr Griffith. But you'll have to give me time.

GRIFFITH You're a good man, Epping. Posterity's going to thank you. Billy...

BITZER *turns back to* GRIFFITH.

Billy, tomorrow I want to shoot a whole army. A whole army on the move!

EPPING } (together) { Mr Griffith!
BITZER }   { D.W.!

GRIFFITH Everyone we can muster, Rose, every actor on the lot. Extras, extras, extras. Get them in from other pictures if you have to, but get me extras.

EPPING *exits, in shock.*

BITZER You'll be wasting your money. They won't look much bigger than jackrabbits.

GRIFFITH Don't underrate things, Billy. Your audience or yourself. Get that lens of yours on a hilltop and shoot a valley in one fell swoop. A whole army, Billy, that's what we'll get. A whole army and then some!

Everyone freezes. The lights dim and they seem like a frozen-frame. **ROSE** *steps in to a spot. The speech and following scene are underscored.*

ROSE So Mr Griffith shot his picture and told his story. And it was the greatest, the biggest, the grandest, the most spectacular event of cinematic history. He called it *The Birth of a Nation*. And he spent ninety thousand dollars. He used one time three hundred extras and he controlled them like a general from the top of a tower. Close-ups. Fade-outs. Iris shots – he invented them all and used them all for his picture. Every technique we've ever seen in a movie since.

LILLIAN *and* **GRIFFITH** *step out of the frozen-frame.* **LILLIAN** *produces a pair of shoes, as if from nowhere.*

LILLIAN Mr Griffith... I have something for you. The new shoes you promised yourself.

GRIFFITH *(taking the shoes)* Box office, Miss Lillian. We've done it.

LILLIAN History written in lightning... So dreams come true after all.

GRIFFITH Life as it's dreamt – just a hair's breadth away. And it's only the beginning.

LILLIAN What?

GRIFFITH We can go on. The same dream, only bigger. They won't call 'em flickers now, Miss Lillian. From today on, they're up there with Michelangelo.

MUSIC 9: "THEY DON'T CALL 'EM FLICKERS"

GRIFFITH And da Vinci and Rembrandt and Shakespeare and...

(singing)
THERE'S A NEW FEELIN' QUITE A NEW FEELIN'
BLOWIN' IN FROM OUTSIDE
SOMETHIN' ALIVE AND WIDE
COMIN' IN ON THE TIDE

The **COMPANY** *unfreeze for* ***"MUSIC 9"***. *Lights revert to normal.*

GIRLS
JOIN IN A NEWBORN WONDERFUL NEW DAWN
COME ALONG FOR THE RIDE

STRONG MALE SOLO
PART OF THE PAST HAS DIED FLICKERS ARE ON THE SLIDE
AND THE MOTION PICTURE BUSINESS HAS REACHED THE
  GREAT DIVIDE

COMPANY
THEY CALLED 'EM FLICKERS BEFORE *THE BIRTH OF A NATION*
WAS SUCH A SENSATIONAL HIT
THAT FILM UNDOUBTEDLY PROVED HOW
THE MOVIES HAVE MOVED NOW
RIGHT INTO A NEW WORLD SO FLICKERS BETTER QUIT!
THE EPIC SCALE OF PRODUCTION THE BRILLIANCE OF
  CONSTRUCTION
WERE SUCH THEY CREATED A FURORE
AND WHEN THE PICTURE WAS DONE A BRAND-NEW ERA HAD
  BEGUN

    AND THEY DON'T CALL 'EM FLICKERS ANY MORE

CAMERAMAN
    THEY CALLED 'EM FLICKERS WAY BACK WHEN *DAN THE
        SHARPSHOOTER*
    WAS HAILED AS A MUTOSCOPE HIT
    TODAY WHEN FILMS ARE COLOSSAL
    THAT PICTURE'S A FOSSIL
    THAT JEST ABOUT MEASURES AS FAR AS YOU C'N SPIT
    THE ACTION'S UNREAL AND JERKY THE LIGHTING'S KINDA
        MURKY
    BUT NOW THANK THE LORD THOSE DAYS ARE GONE
    WE'RE ALL PROFESSIONALS NOW SINCE DAVID GRIFFITH
        TAUGHT US HOW
    AND WE AIN'T SHOOTIN' FLICKERS FROM NOW ON

OLD STUDIO HAND
    WE CALLED 'EM FLICKERS BACK WHEN A SEAT COST A NICKEL
    WITH SLAP AND A TICKLE THROWN IN
    WHERE ONCE AN OUT-OF-TUNE PIANNER
    PLAYED "STAR-SPANGLED BANNER"
    A FANCY ORCHESTRA'S PERFORMING "LOHENGRIN"
    AND NOW A SEAT COSTS A DOLLAR YOU WEAR A TIE AND
        COLLAR
    AND CHECK IN YOUR HEADGEAR AT THE DOOR
    THESE BIG NEW FLICKERS LOOK SMART AND WHAT'S MORE
        GRIFFITH SAYS THEY'RE ART
    SO WE DAREN'T CALL THEM FLICKERS ANY MORE

COMPANY
    THEY CALLED 'EM FLICKERS BEFORE *THE BIRTH OF A NATION*
    BECAME A SENSATIONAL SMASH
    THE DAY THAT PICTURE EXPLODED
    THE REST WERE OUTMODED
    THE NEW GRIFFITH TECHNIQUE HAD SHOWN 'EM UP AS
        TRASH
    THOSE AVANT-GARDE INNOVATIONS THOSE OFF-THE-CUFF
        CREATIONS
    WERE NOT EVER IN THE BOOK BEFORE

TILL HE TURNED OVER THE PAGE AND MOTION PICTURES
   CAME OF AGE
AND THEY DON'T CALL 'EM FLICKERS
THEY DON'T TALK OF FLICKERS
'COS THERE AREN'T ANY FLICKERS ANY MORE

There is a blackout.

Light rises on **LILLIAN** *and* **MOMMA GISH**.

MOMMA Lillian, there are riots. From Boston in the North to Alabama in the South.

LILLIAN But why, Momma?

MOMMA Because of *Birth of a Nation*. They say that Mr Griffith is no friend of the black man.

LILLIAN No!

MOMMA They say he portrays black men as fools and the Klu Klux Klan as heroes.

LILLIAN No! He's just being true to history.

MOMMA Are you sure, Lillian?

LILLIAN I...

MOMMA Lillian, are you sure?

Light fades on them as a spot rises on **MAN OF THE SOUTH**.

MUSIC 10: "RIVERS OF BLOOD"

MAN
   MOVIE MAN MOVIE MAN
   LOOK WHAT YOU'VE DONE
   LOOK WHAT YOUR PICTURES
   AND ALL HAVE BEGUN
   NOW ON THE WHITE OF THE KLANSMAN'S HOOD
   THERE WILL BE RIVERS OF BLOOD
   THERE WILL BE RIVERS OF BLOOD

MOVIE MAN MOVIE MAN
HEED WHAT WE SAY
HERE IN THE SOUTH
THERE IS TROUBLE TODAY
HERE IN THE COTTON FIELDS STAINING THE MUD
THERE WILL BE RIVERS OF BLOOD

THERE WILL BE RIVERS OF BLOOD

LOOK WHAT YOU'VE DONE WITH YOUR
FLICKERING LIGHT
YOUR PURE SCREEN OF SILVER
BRINGS FEAR IN THE NIGHT
WHAT HAVE YOU DONE WITH YOUR TRUMPETS
AND SONG?
YOU'VE DONE US WRONG

MOVIE MAN MOVE MAN
STAY FROM OUR DOOR
WE DON'T WANT NO PART OF
YOUR TROUBLE IN STORE
WHAT IS A TRICKLE WILL SOON BE A FLOOD
TURNING TO RIVERS OF BLOOD

TURNING TO RIVERS OF BLOOD

The spot fades.

MUSIC 10(A): "WORKIN' IN FLICKERS" - Reprise

The lights come up. The camera has been cleared in the darkness and a desk has been set for **ZUKOR**.

ZUKOR *enters and sits at the desk.*

MARY *(offstage)* It's my birthday, Mr Zukor.

ZUKOR I know, my dear. Happy twelfth birthday.

MARY *runs on.*

I have a surprise for you.

MARY A present? For me?

ZUKOR *(coming down the stairs)* Come to the window, Mary.

MARY What's always this with the window?

ZUKOR *(leading her)* Close your eyes... turn around... open them.

MARY *(crestfallen)* Oh...

ZUKOR Your picture! Twenty storeys high!

MARY Thank you. *(She goes to the top of the stairs, then turns back)* I'm always the little girl, Mr Zukor. Why won't you let me grow up?

ZUKOR You're the most famous little girl in the world.

MARY I'm twenty-one.

ZUKOR The American movie industry is...

MARY ...in the palm of my pudgy hand... I know, I read my own press.

ZUKOR Mary, your sleeves *are* a little short, my dear. We don't want you catching cold.

MARY goes to sit on ZUKOR's desk.

MARY Oh dear, Mr Zukor. I'm sure we have the same ideas, you and me. We just express them different... And besides, Momma's sure of you, so... It's just that, when I should have been, I was never allowed to be a little girl. I've had to earn a living since I was so high. Without a Poppa, well...it was up to me to keep the family together. So I must be with people Momma's sure of. I've become the little girl I was never allowed to be and...

ZUKOR ...and now, my dear, you've got to become even younger. You know your Momma's done a survey?

MARY She told me.

ZUKOR She couldn't fail to notice that the further away you get from "Little Mary" – I'm using her words, my dear – the further away you get from "Little Mary", the greater the drop in the box office take. She thinks you've got to be even more American, that your curls should get even longer, and that you should grow younger still.

MARY She mentioned money, I suppose.

ZUKOR I have never had a conversation with your mother, Mary, when she has not mentioned money.

MARY She's on your side – you should pay her more than me. She'd have them down to my ankles if she could!

ZUKOR And does the public agree! I've just had my returns. *Rebecca of Sunnybrook Farm* has grossed a million in a month.

MARY Well, what more could they want? Nobody ever lived in a world like I do in that picture. Roses round the front gate – all year long. Horses and buggies and church-home-and-schoolroom. It couldn't fail.

ZUKOR And it's pure Mary Pickford.

MARY *(very sweetly)* I think that's why Momma's asking for seven hundred thousand. *(She pauses)* A year, of course.

ZUKOR To everyone else I'm a big shot movie mogul. To you and your momma I'm a dollar machine. I think of that, my dear, whenever I incline to pride.

MARY *(jumping off the desk)* Do you know, Mr Zukor, I have a dream. I'm going to live it out one day. First I go to the hairdresser and have my hair cut really short. Then I get myself a dress. Something that's a bit low at the front and doesn't have a frill in sight. And without the hair and the vegetable rinse and the make-up I don't look particularly young or particularly appealing or special at all really, so I don't have to watch what I say and who I say it to and what I do and who I do it with. Isn't it a lovely dream?

ZUKOR *(going to her)* A dream it'll stay, my dear. Unless you want to lose your place.

MARY No, I don't want to lose my place. *(She has caught sight of the picture again. Quietly now)* That's the trouble, isn't it?

ZUKOR Then stay the way you are. A little girl in her own front parlour.

MARY Yes, Mr Zukor. You always know what's best for me.

ZUKOR and MARY clasp little fingers; then MARY starts to go.

ZUKOR *(shaking his head)* Ah, ah... Time for a press conference, don't you think, my dear? *(He claps his hands – once)*

The PRESSMEN appear, as if from nowhere.

MARY produces an instant smile.

Gentlemen, I am proud to make an announcement. Paramount Pictures has today signed a new contract with its biggest, brightest star.

The PRESSMEN applaud.

Miss Mary Pickford.

The PRESSMEN applaud.

(signalling for more applause) For seven hundred thousand a year.

PRESSMAN 1 But Mr Zukor – that's more than they pay the President of the United States.

ZUKOR It's more than they pay me.

PRESSMAN 2 And do you think this money will change Miss Pickford?

ZUKOR Gentlemen, Miss Pickford is part of the American way of life. I assure you that no amount of money will ever change Little Mary.

*The introduction to **"MUSIC 11"** begins.*

ZUKOR *exits.*

MARY *begins her song, closely attended by two members of the studio publicity department.*

MUSIC 11: "I LIKE TO BE THE WAY I AM IN MY OWN FRONT PARLOUR"

MARY *(speaking)* Hello!

PRESS *(speaking)* Hello!

Singing.
I LIKE TO BE THE WAY I AM IN MY OWN FRONT PARLOUR
A LITTLE GIRL WHO'S INNOCENT AND NAIVE
I HAVEN'T GOT AN AWFUL LOT OF ANYTHING OF VALUE
EXCEPT OF COURSE A HEART OF GOLD AND THAT IS ON MY SLEEVE
I'M JUST A HEALTHY OUTDOOR GIRL WITH A FEW FRECKLES
A KID WHOSE HAIR HAS GOT A NATURAL CURL
I DON'T USE SCENT OR MAKE-UP OR PUT POWDER WHERE MY FACE IS
I DON'T DRESS UP IN FANCY CLOTHES OR PUT ON AIRS, AND GRACES
I'D RATHER SHOP AT FIVE-AND-TEN THAN SPEND A LOT AT MACY'S
I'M JUST A WHOLESOME SIMPLE LITTLE GIRL

PUBLICISTS
    EVERYWHERE SHE GOES
    WE GO
    PROTECTING HER EGO
    FROM THE WICKED WORLD OUTSIDE

MARY
    I LIKE TO BE THE WAY I AM

PUBLICISTS
    IN THIS KINDA PRESS
    SCRIMMAGE

ACT I

PROJECTING HER IMAGE
TO HER PUBLIC NATIONWIDE

PRESS
SHE LIKES TO BE THE WAY
   SHE IS
IN HER OWN FRONT ROOM
SHE LIKES TO BE LITTLE
   AND NAIVE
AND WEAR HER GOLDEN
   HEART UPON HER SLEEVE
SHE'S SO HEALTHY LIVING
   OUTDOORS
JUST LOOK AT ALL THOSE
   FRECKLES AND CURLS
YOU KNOW SHE WON'T USE
   MAKE-UP AND SHE WON'T
   USE SCENT
SHE DON'T GO FOR AIRS AND
   GRACES
PLACES LIKE MACY'S SHE
   DON'T CARE TO GO
SHE'S JUST A WHOLESOME
   GIRL

MARY
I DO I DO

MARY
I DON'T APPEAR AT GRAUMAN'S IN A PLATINUM TIARA
BUT IF I DID I WOULDN'T BE LIKE DARLING THEDA BARA
WHO'S NEVER SEEN A SINGLE FILM BECAUSE OF HER
   MASCARA

MARY/PRESS
I'M JUST A HOMESPUN ORDINARY NEXT-DOOR APPLE-PIE
   REGULAR SIMPLE LITTLE GIRL

Everyone exits, leaving **MARY** *alone on stage.*

As soon as she is alone **MARY** *envelops herself in a most luxurious fur coat.*

MARY *exits – a star.*

    LILLIAN *enters from the other side.*

LILLIAN *(to the* AUDIENCE*)* Can you believe it? I mean... you must've heard the talk. Nobody knew what to expect next from Mr Griffith. But what they didn't expect was this.*(She becomes confidential)* He's making a little picture. Nothing much more than one of those flickers he hated so much in the early days. No big sets. No action scenes. Just a little old thing about a man in jail who's condemned to die for a crime he didn't do. He says it's about...

    BITZER *enters left and crosses the set.*

BITZER ...tyranny.

LILLIAN Tyranny - yes.

    BITZER *exits right.*

    ROSE *enters left and crosses the set.*

ROSE He's making a new movie.

LILLIAN I know. About a man in jail.

ROSE He's finished that. This is another one. A costume piece about...

LILLIAN ...tyranny?

ROSE Tyranny. In the sixteenth century.

    ROSE *exits right.*

    SENNETT *enters left, crossing the set.*

SENNETT He starts a new picture. Shooting today.

LILLIAN About tyranny?

SENNETT You've got it. The worst one of the lot. Jesus. The Gospels. Matthew, Mark, Luke and...

LILLIAN He hasn't released the other two yet.

ACT I

SENNETT He's up to something. You mark my words.

SENNETT *exits right.*

GRIFFITH *enters left.*

LILLIAN Mr Griffith...

GRIFFITH I'm going to make a picture.

LILLIAN Of course you are, Mr Griffith, but...

GRIFFITH *The Birth of a Nation* – they tried to ban it, you know. How can it be allowed – such intolerance?

LILLIAN Look, Mr Griffith...

GRIFFITH That's what it'll be about, my new picture. And you gave me the idea yourself.

LILLIAN I did?

GRIFFITH Life as it is. That's the biggest battle of them all. Bigger than the Civil War – it's man's own war. His war against himself. Man as his own worst enemy. His tyranny. His intolerance. That's what I'm going to do. And I aim to set my story in ancient Babylon.

LILLIAN But...

GRIFFITH I have a little something up my sleeve.

ROSE *enters.*

ROSE Mr Griffith, there's a fellow outside to see you. He says his name's "Spec".

GRIFFITH It is.

LILLIAN Spec?

GRIFFITH Short for "perspective". He's a scenic designer. The best of the century.

ROSE But we've never used a designer before.

GRIFFITH We've never made a picture like this before. *(He brings the* **TWO GIRLS** *to him, almost whispering)* That fellow out there is Walter L. Hall.

LILLIAN *and* **ROSE** *look blank.*

Why ladies, he's the greatest realiser of dreams in the world today.

ROSE *(as she goes)* After you, Mr Griffith.

GRIFFITH After me, of course.

ROSE *exits.*

LILLIAN Why do you need a man like...?

GRIFFITH Spec. I need him because he's going to plan for me the biggest movie set in history. Past or future.

LILLIAN You can't account for the future.

GRIFFITH I can have a damn good try. *(He holds her)* Three stories, Miss Lillian – and now a fourth. On a scale no dreamer has dreamt of before.

LILLIAN But why four? Wouldn't one be enough?

GRIFFITH That's what I'll have in the end. Four stories. One movie.

LILLIAN One story per movie is the norm, Mr Griffith.

GRIFFITH *Was* the norm. Before cross-cutting.

LILLIAN I don't understand what that is, I'm afraid.

GRIFFITH You will, Miss Gish. You will.

ROSE *returns with* **SPEC**, *a round man of very few words who carries a drawing board under his arm.*

Mr Hall...

SPEC Spec.

GRIFFITH Spec. *(He puts an arm around* **SPEC***)* I want you to rebuild Babylon for me.

There is a pause.

SPEC That should be simple enough.

LILLIAN *(going to* **SPEC***)* I don't think you understand. He means life-size.

GRIFFITH No, my dear – I mean larger-than-life. *(He gestures out front)* Walls a hundred feet high. Towers so tall you see 'em from the other end of Sunset Boulevard. Elephants.

SPEC *(starting to write on his board)* I'll need to know the title, Mr Griffith. What's your picture to be called?

They hold their breath

GRIFFITH I'm going to say it as it is. My picture's called *Intolerance.*

SPEC *scribbles on his board and turns away with* **ROSE**. **GRIFFITH** *crosses down with* **LILLIAN**.

EPPING *enters and looks worriedly over* **SPEC**'s *shoulder.*

This is it, Miss Lillian. I'm rebuilding Babylon for you. That's a big enough thing to build, don't you think?

EPPING *(looking at the board)* ...Elephants!?

GRIFFITH *sees* **EPPING** *approaching and makes a hasty exit.*

Mr Griff... He's biting off a hell of a chunk with this one, Miss Gish.

LILLIAN If it's good they'll all be doing it next year.

EPPING But the top of those walls'll be as wide as roads. Two chariots'll pass with room to spare.

ROSE *(coming down) And* he's paying five dollars to any extra who'll jump off 'em!

LILLIAN Let's hope he's got enough nets to catch them all.

EPPING Let's hope he's got enough money to pay them all. *(He pauses)* None of you will be named, you know.

LILLIAN Mr Griffith never names his players. He likes us to be anonymous. That's his policy and always has been.

EPPING Oh, a wise move in the past maybe...but now? People are getting to want stars, Miss Gish. People are getting to want to know the names behind the most famous faces in the world.

GRIFFITH *and* **BITZER** *enter.*

BITZER You're asking me to *fly*, D.W. You want me to shoot the whole of your set at once then swoop in on one tiny detail. I'd have to be a bird to do that, and even you can't give me wings.

GRIFFITH But I can give you a balloon, Billy. And with one big balloon you can fly your camera through Babylon like an eagle.

EPPING *nearly has a seizure – and exits.*

BITZER *(running after* **EPPING***)* Don't worry – I'll get a second-hand balloon.

BITZER *exits.*

GRIFFITH *crosses to take* **LILLIAN***'s hand.*

GRIFFITH Do you read your Bible?

LILLIAN Naturally.

GRIFFITH So you'll know what happened to the Tower of Babel.

LILLIAN *(with a smile)* Immigrant labour?

GRIFFITH Language – that's what happened. A damn good project ruined because one fellow didn't know what the

ACT I

next was saying. What a way to run a world. *(Then he smiles too)* Miss Lillian...

LILLIAN Mr Griffith.

GRIFFITH It's got to succeed, Lillian. It's just got to.

The **COMPANY** *enters.*

GRIFFITH *turns, his confidence restored.* *"MUSIC 12" is addressed out to the* **AUDIENCE***, as if towards the site of his* Intolerance *set.*

MUSIC 12: "BEYOND BABEL"

(speaking) Ladies and gentlemen, you know what this means? This talk of flickers and moving pictures – you know where it's leading? It's taking us beyond words... beyond Babel to a...

(singing)
UNIVERSAL LANGUAGE
A POWER THAT CAN MAKE MEN BROTHERS
A MULTI-LINGUAL MESSAGE OF LOVE AND PEACE TO OTHERS

THIS IS THE DREAM I DREAM MY FRIENDS
THIS IS THE MAGIC MACHINE MY FRIENDS
TO MAKE THE DREAM MY SILVER DREAM REALITY

BEYOND BABEL BEYOND WORDS
SILENT AND YET HEARD
SUDDENLY THE OLD IDEAL
THAT WE'VE DREAMED ABOUT IS REAL
A SILENT LANGUAGE THE WORLD CAN UNDERSTAND
IS AT HAND

BEYOND BABEL BEYOND DREAMS
ON THE HORIZON THE PROMISED VISION GLEAMS
NOW THROUGH THE MIST WE CAN MAKE OUT
ALL THAT THE FUTURE CAN BE
THIS IS THE MOMENT WE BREAK OUT
HERE IS A VOICE WE CAN SEE
BEYOND SOUND BEYOND WORDS BEYOND BABEL

GRIFFITH and **COMPANY**
BEYOND BABEL BEYOND WORDS
SILENT AND YET HEARD
SUDDENLY THE OLD IDEAL
THAT WE'VE DREAMED ABOUT IS REAL
A SILENT LANGUAGE THE WORLD CAN UNDERSTAND

GRIFFITH
IS AT HAND

GRIFFITH	**COMPANY**
BEYOND BABEL BEYOND DREAMS	BABEL
ON THE HORIZON THE PROMISED VISION GLEAMS	
NOW THROUGH THE MIST WE CAN MAKE OUT	NOW WE CAN SEE
ALL THAT THE FUTURE CAN BE	NOW WE CAN SEE HIS DREAM
THIS IS THE MOMENT WE BREAK OUT	WE UNDERSTAND HIS DREAM
HERE IS A VOICE WE CAN SEE	

GRIFFITH and **COMPANY**
BEYOND SOUND
BEYOND WORDS
BEYOND BABEL BEYOND BABEL BEYOND BABEL
BEYOND BABEL BEYOND BABEL

End of ACT ONE

ACT II

The Act opens in darkness. **ROSE** *and the* **COMPANY** *are on stage.*

MUSIC 13: "A DAVID GRIFFITH SHOW"

A single spot comes up on **ROSE**.

ROSE Ladies and gentlemen, you are invited to the trade preview of *Intolerance*... Your comment forms await you in the foyer... The picture begins in the blinking of an eye...

The lights expand to reveal the **MOVIEGOERS** *sitting on the steps dressed in smart evening dress. Two prominent advertising boards announce INTOLERANCE – TRADE PREVIEW*

COMPANY *(singing)*
WE'VE SEEN *BIRTH OF A NATION* THAT ONE SPILT SOME BLOOD
NOW HIS LATEST CREATION SURE WON'T BE A DUD
THIS ONE YOU CAN BE CERTAIN WON'T SINK IN THE MUD
WHY HELL IT'S A DAVID GRIFFITH SHOW

A **NEWSBOY** *crosses at the back of the steps.*

NEWSBOY *(speaking)* "*Lusitania*" Torpedoed! One Hundred Americans Killed by Boche!

A few of the **MEN** *break away from the* **COMPANY** *and leave the set.*

COMPANY *(singing)*
WE'RE SO LUCKY TO SIT HERE SAYING "THIS IS ART"
THERE IS DRAMA AND WIT HERE FROM THE VERY START
THIS WILL GET IN TO EVERY MOVING PICTURE CHART

WHY HELL IT'S A DAVID GRIFFITH SHOW

The **NEWSBOY** *crosses back.*

NEWSBOY *(speaking)* Edith Cavell Shot by German Firing Squad! Belgian Babies Slain!

More of the **COMPANY** *break away and leave the set.*

COMPANY *(singing)*
WE IN HOLLYWOOD SAW THOSE
WALLS OF BABYLON
WITH THE RABBLE ON TOP
DON'T DOUBT HIM
HE WAS HERE WAY BEFORE THOSE
DOUBTING THOMASES
SAID HIS PROMISE WOULD STOP THEY'D HAVE A FLOP
WITHOUT HIM

The **NEWSBOY** *crosses for the final time.*

NEWSBOY *(speaking)* Draft Parades in 'Frisco! America Joins the War!

The **COMPANY** *now filter out one by one, until a* **SOLE FEMALE VOICE** *is left to finish the number.*

COMPANY *(singing; diminishing in numbers)*
WHEN YOU THINK WHAT HE'S SPENDING IT MUST BE A CERT
REAL-LIFE WONDERFUL ENDING HE'LL GET BACK HIS SHIRT
HE'LL SING SWEET FOR THE BACKERS NO ONE WILL BE HURT

SOLO FEMALE *(half-spoken)* Why hell it's a David Griffith show.

The **GIRL** *walks off, self-consciously.*

MARY, GRIFFITH, LILLIAN *and* **ZUKOR** *pass her at the exit.*

LILLIAN You've done it, Mr Griffith. You've made *Intolerance* the greatest movie ever.

GRIFFITH Thank you. You're wrong.

LILLIAN I can't be, Mr Griffith. That movie's real.

GRIFFITH There's something more real. It's called the Great War and it's happening in Europe now.

LILLIAN That's five thousand miles away.

MARY It's right here in this theatre.

LILLIAN Not you, Mary. I thought you'd see sense at least.

MARY I can see he's made a picture about peace and tolerance when half the country's itching to get off and fight.

LILLIAN That's not fair.

GRIFFITH Fair? If I could've stopped America going to war I would have burned every print of that movie and forgot it ever happened.

ZUKOR Be careful what you wish for. You may get it.

LILLIAN I don't believe I'm hearing this. You've all gone crazy.

MARY *Intolerance* isn't the kind of picture they'll want to see right now.

LILLIAN You heard *that* audience. They loved it.

MARY An invited audience, Lillian. What about the public?

LILLIAN Mr Griffith pleases his public. Tell them, Mr Griffith... tell them I'm right.

ZUKOR They don't want to be preached at any more. They want escapism.

LILLIAN He makes good pictures.

GRIFFITH Miss Lillian...

MARY *(taking his arm)* Of course you make good pictures, D.W. You just got lousy timing.

LILLIAN Now listen...

MARY No – you listen, Lillian. There's more of you in this picture than any you've ever played in before. And this time on the production side. You've talked about nothing else since it started. You've lived, slept, eaten and breathed *Intolerance*.

GRIFFITH Mary – she even sewed the costumes.

LILLIAN And I'd do it again. I had faith in it. I still do. I was in the darkroom there...cutting...picking takes. You took me into your confidence.

GRIFFITH It was my picture.

LILLIAN I'm wondering...if perhaps you'd exploited your stars, you might...

GRIFFITH Stars! So that's it! You want to be another Mary Pickford!

MARY She couldn't, D.W. There's only one.

There is a pause.

GRIFFITH I swear to you, Miss Pickford, that if it takes me the rest of my life I will pay back every penny I owe on this picture.

MARY Your advisors will tell you: legally there's no need.

GRIFFITH Your memory will tell you: Griffith deals in morals.

GRIFFITH *strides from the set.*

MARY Leave him, Lillian.

LILLIAN Now? He's on the crest of a wave.

ZUKOR His picture's going to bomb. He owes his backers.

LILLIAN But...

MARY I know about these things. Leave him. You're a star now yourself.

LILLIAN He doesn't believe in that sort of thing.

MARY But you should. You owe it to yourself. To your career.

LILLIAN He gave me my career.

MARY You must think of number one.

LILLIAN I am. Him.

The music for **"MORE THAN A MAN"** *begins.* **MARY** *and* **ZUKOR** *move out of focus.*

MUSIC 14: "MORE THAN A MAN"
MAYBE HE TRIES TOO HARD
MAYBE HE FLIES TOO HIGH
I KNOW HE'LL NEVER QUIT UNTIL
HE LEARNS THE WHERE AND WHY
OF A CLOUD OR A TREE
OR WHAT MAKES THE EARTH AND THE SEA
AND HOW CAN MEN BE AS FREE
AS THE STARS IN THE SKY

MAYBE HE WORKS TOO LONG
MAYBE HE SLEEPS TOO LIGHT
FOR A MAN WITH A HEAD FULL OF DREAMS
AND A BEAUTIFUL PLAN
YET HE'S ONLY A MAN
WHO'S MORE THAN A MAN

At the end of the number, **LILLIAN** *moves away.* **MARY** *and* **ZUKOR** *come back into focus.*

ZUKOR Accountants were invented to write off debts. Why doesn't he just get on with making pictures?

MARY Don't write Griffith off yet, Mr Zukor. I haven't.

ZUKOR Charity, Mary? From you?

MARY No – sense. You know all about that...you're the head of Paramount.

ZUKOR And you are my greatest star. Think what we mean to each other – Paramount and Pickford.

MARY Pickford and Paramount.

ZUKOR The sentiment's the same.

There is a pause.

MARY Forgive me.

ZUKOR What for?

MARY I'm leaving.

ZUKOR Who?

MARY You.

ZUKOR What?

MARY I mean it, Mr Zukor. I'm leaving my Paramount home.

ZUKOR But Mary, I've been like a father to you.

MARY I didn't need one. My Momma was both parents wrapped up in one.

***MUSIC 14(A): "I LIKE TO BE THE WAY I AM"** - Reprise*

The music begins slowly, underlining the following dialogue.

ZUKOR I looked out for you when you were a little girl. In ringlets and frills.

MARY There was gold in them thar frills.

ZUKOR A little girl, Mary.

MARY Look at me – I still am.

ZUKOR A little girl with a dream?

MARY Oh, I've still got that dream all right.

ZUKOR You sound like Griffith.

MARY No. Mine's the sort that comes true.

ZUKOR That's what he says.

MARY He lives in a world of his own. I live in this one.

ZUKOR And in this world dreams come true?

MARY Flashback, Mr Zukor. Remember what I said. Short hair. A grown-up dress. Privacy. Freedom. All the things that are in my power. Not Griffith's. Not God's. Mine.

ZUKOR You wouldn't dare.

MARY Don't tempt me.

The music becomes louder.

ZUKOR It'd mean the end of everything. Of your career. The end of you.

MARY Haven't you heard, Mr Zukor? A career's just a beam of light.

ZUKOR That's all a star is, Mary. A beam of light to us mere mortals.

MARY You're not mortal, Mr Zukor.

ZUKOR Yes, even me. But not you.

The music is louder still now, and more in tempo.

You are worshipped, Mary. That's what it comes to now. Your picture on the altar in the Cathedral of Light. From Michigan to Moscow. From Paris to Pittsburgh. Not the Madonna, Miss Pickford, though the name's the same. Not the Virgin Mary. Mary the movie star. Paramount's Mary.

The music stops.

(speaking quietly) Remember that…next time your head touches the pillow.

ZUKOR *exits.*

MARY *waits a moment then sings the final verse of* "MUSIC 14(A)". *As she sings, she peels off the little girl dress and wig to reveal a sophisticated gown and shingled hair.*

MARY *(singing)*

AT LAST IT'S TIME TO LIVE MY DREAM TO CUT MY CURLS AND GROW UP
IF ZUKOR CALLS ME CHILD AGAIN THERE'S GONNA BE A BLOW-UP
AND IF I SEE ANOTHER FRILL I SWEAR I'M GONNA THROW UP
'COS NOW YOU SEE A
COPPER-PLATED SVELTE AND SMART SOPHISTICATED
SELF-SUPPORTING LIBERATED GIRL

There is a blackout.

Single spots rise on **ROSE** *and* **EPPING**, *one extreme right, the other extreme left.*

ROSE How much does he owe, Mr Epping?

EPPING Close on a million dollars.

ROSE And the movie's a disaster?

EPPING He's wandering the theatres...barking his shins on empty seats.

ROSE Poetry?

EPPING No, despair. I'm just a money-man, Rose – why did this have to happen?

ROSE It's a different world.

EPPING He always said it would be.

ROSE I don't think this is quite what he had in mind.

EPPING You know about the new company?

ROSE Rumours. Tell me more.

EPPING They're all joining up. Pickford and Fairbanks and Chaplin and...Griffith. They're going into business together. The motion picture business.

ROSE What the hell does she want from him?

EPPING Integrity.

ROSE So the see-saw's come down on Mary's side.

EPPING No, the carousel's turned. Griffith's just along for the ride.

ROSE Griffith's staying put. Something else is moving on.

EPPING Mary?

ROSE Hollywood. Just Hollywood.

The lights expand to reveal the **COMPANY**, *dressed for a tango.* **ROSE** *leads the* **COMPANY** *number.*

MUSIC 15: "THE INDUSTRY"

Singing.
THERE ARE FACTORIES IN THE FOOTHILLS WHERE THE LUPINS USED TO BLOOM
NOW NOTHING GROWS BUT STUDIOS FOR THE CAMERAS TO ZOOM

COMPANY *(singing)*
WE CALL IT THE INDUSTRY AND WE'RE VERY PROUD TO SAY
THE INDUSTRY HAS NO TIME FOR YESTERDAY
THE PUBLIC DON'T WANT ART AND IT'S THE PUBLIC WE MUST PLEASE
A DOUBLE DOSE OF HEART DON'T RAISE COMPLETION GUARANTEES
EACH DAY IN THE INDUSTRY THE ONLY THING WE NEED TO KNOW
IS THAT A PROFIT IS THE ONLY THING WE NEED TO SHOW
DON'T COME TO HOLLYWOOD AND SAY YOU WANNA BE A STAR
WITHOUT THE INDUSTRY YOU AIN'T GOING VERY FAR

ROSE *(singing)*
I REMEMBER LIFE IN THE FOOTHILLS WHEN THE STARS WERE KIDS AT PLAY
BUT NOW THE GAME IS NOT THE SAME IT HAS RULES YOU MUST OBEY

Add one **GIRL** *– top voice.*

NOW EACH SUNNY DAY IN THE FOOTHILLS EVERY WORKER IS EMPLOYED
TO MANUFACTURE DREAMS AND WRAP 'EM UP IN CELLULOID

MEN
THE TROUBLE WITH THESE DREAMS IS THAT YOU HAVE TO KEEP AWAKE
HERE IN THE INDUSTRY EVERYONE IS ON THE MAKE

GIRLS
MEN *(together)*
SO THE FACTORIES IN THE FOOTHILLS BECOME TEMPLES TO THE LAW
THE LAW THAT STATES THAT MOVIE DATES MUST GROSS YOU MORE AND MORE
SO HERE'S TO THE INDUSTRY THAT STANDS FOR "NOW" INSTEAD OF "THEN"
THE INDUSTRY WELCOME TO THE LION'S DEN

The **COMPANY** *clears.*

LILLIAN *is left alone.*

GRIFFITH *enters and crosses the stage without seeming to see her.*

LILLIAN Mr Griffith?

GRIFFITH Not now, Lillian. I'm really very busy.

LILLIAN Too busy for me?

GRIFFITH Of course not, my dear. I'm thinking, that's all.

LILLIAN About money?

GRIFFITH Whatever gave you that idea?

LILLIAN You owe rather a lot. At least, that's what they're saying.

GRIFFITH Gossip!

LILLIAN All the same...

GRIFFITH All the same, nothing. I owe some money. But I'm going to pay it back.

LILLIAN If you don't mind my asking – how?

GRIFFITH By making more pictures, of course.

LILLIAN What kind of pictures, Mr Griffith?

GRIFFITH My kind. Is there any other?

LILLIAN That's something else they're saying too. That there's a new kind of picture.

GRIFFITH None that I know of.

LILLIAN But...

GRIFFITH Do *you* know of a new kind of picture, Miss Lillian?

LILLIAN Not exactly, but...

GRIFFITH I don't think you're telling me the truth. We don't lie to each other, do we?

LILLIAN Of course not, Mr Griffith.

GRIFFITH Then out with it. I thought I'd learned a thing or two about the movies. Obviously I was wrong.

LILLIAN It's not the pictures that are changing so much, it's...

GRIFFITH Well?

LILLIAN There's a different sort of feel to things. A different sort of scent in the air.

GRIFFITH You mean I'm old-fashioned.

LILLIAN I mean you deal in morals.

GRIFFITH I thought that's what *we* dealt in, Miss Lillian.

LILLIAN I follow wherever you lead, Mr Griffith – you know that.

GRIFFITH But suddenly I'm leading you up blind alleyways?

LILLIAN Suddenly you need to accept a little help. We all do, Mr Griffith. None of us can work in isolation any more. The industry...

GRIFFITH Industry!

LILLIAN The industry's expanding. We depend on each other, but more than that – we depend on our audiences.

GRIFFITH I know my audience.

LILLIAN Do you, Mr Griffith? John Doe's been away fighting a war. Now he's come back he wants something different.

GRIFFITH You mean "stars", I suppose?

LILLIAN Stars are only a part of it.

GRIFFITH Your name means as much to the public as mine, Lillian...maybe you're right.

LILLIAN That's not what I meant.

GRIFFITH Maybe you should capitalize on it. Maybe you should go off on your own.

LILLIAN That's not what I meant.

There is a pause.

GRIFFITH *(quietly)* Of course it isn't. I'm sorry, Miss Gish, I've offended you.

LILLIAN I was trying to offer some help, that's all.

GRIFFITH I'm not in need of any. Just at the moment. *(tenderly)* Miss Lillian, I mean it. You'd be better off by yourself. The way money is now I can't afford to pay you what you're worth. I'm thinking in your own interest.

LILLIAN My interests are yours, Mr Griffith.

GRIFFITH You must look after yourself, my dear.

There is a pause.

LILLIAN *(choking back tears)* Congratulations are in order, I hear.

GRIFFITH For me?

LILLIAN And Mary and the others... Your new company, Mr Griffith.

GRIFFITH Oh, that.

LILLIAN Sounds like a pretty big deal to me.

GRIFFITH Distribution and exhibition, Miss Lillian. The usual thing.

LILLIAN What are you going to call it?

GRIFFITH United Artists. *(He pauses)* An example of that co-operation you were talking about.

LILLIAN I wish you well.

GRIFFITH And me you. God bless you, Miss Lillian.

LILLIAN Godspeed... David.

    LILLIAN *exits.*

MUSIC 15: "THE INDUSTRY"

MUSIC 16: "GENTLE FADE"

GRIFFITH *(singing)*
    THE COLOURING IS AUTUMN
    THE INGÉNUE IS SAD
    AND NOW THE FAREWELL SCENES ARE BEING PLAYED
    THERE'S A WELL-KNOWN PHRASE FOR MOMENTS SUCH AS
        THESE
    WE START TO EASE
    INTO A GENTLE FADE

    THE SUMMER SEASON'S OVER
    BUT STILL I HEAR THE SOUND
    OF MUSIC FROM THE PICTURE HOUSE ARCADE
    AS A PIANO PLAYS THE HEROINE'S REPRISE

WE START TO EASE
INTO A GENTLE FADE

IN THE EARLY DAYS WE MADE SUCH MAGIC
IT SEEMED TO US THE WORLD WAS IN ITS YOUTH
BUT SOMEWHERE ON THE WAY WE LOST THE MAGIC
DID I STUMBLE IN MY SEARCH FOR TRUTH?

THE TOWN IS NEARLY EMPTY
THE CAROUSEL HAS GONE
AND ALL THE FAREWELL GESTURES HAVE BEEN MADE
NOVEMBER RAIN IS DRIPPING FROM THE TREES
AND SO WE EASE
INTO A GENTLE FADE

THE STORY'S NEARLY OVER
WE'VE REACHED THE FINAL REEL
AND NOW AS WE DESCRIBE IT IN THE TRADE
"AT CURTAIN FALL THROUGH TEARS THE AUDIENCE SEES
A GRADUAL EASE
INTO A GENTLE FADE"

GRIFFITH *is swallowed in a spot fade.*

The lights rise on **ROSE** *and the new-look* **MARY**.

ROSE Mary, I'm so glad you're coming to my party.

MARY You're the Hollywood Hostess, Rose. If I don't come they'll think you didn't ask me.

ROSE Come because you want to, Mary.

MARY I want to. What time do you begin?

ROSE Eight.

MARY Then I'll arrive close on nine. In time to upstage Swanson and steal Astor's keylight. You know what I require?

ROSE I think so.

MARY Stairs. You got stairs?

ROSE I got stairs.

ACT II 63

MARY Well, I come in at the top and hover for ten seconds... fifteen, if I can get away with it. Then I need the men. Can you manage half a dozen?

ROSE *(making notes)* Half a dozen? ...Yes.

MARY They stand on the steps. Three either side. When they get up there the people know I'm coming and they sort of clear a space.

ROSE Why?

MARY They don't want me walking over them. I come down those steps with my eyes on the horizon and God help anyone who stands in my way.

ROSE You learn that trick from Griffith?

There is a pause.

MARY See you at nine.

She turns to go. **ROSE** *follows her.*

ROSE Men and a staircase. Are you sure that's enough?

MARY Ample, Rosie. I do the rest.

MARY *exits.*

ROSE *(looking at her notebook, then out front)* Me – the Hollywood Hostess. When I think back it seems like it was –

MUSIC 17: "ONE LONG PARTY"

Singing.
ONE LONG PARTY
THROUGH THE TWENTIES
WE WERE TEMPTING FATE
WE ALL STAYED ON
TILL THE PARTY ENDED
IN NINETEEN-TWENTY-EIGHT

THE PARTY BEGAN

AT THE START OF THE DECADE
WHEN DECADENCE STARTED A SCARE
WITH THAT NEAR-THE-KNUCKLE
FATTY ARBUCKLE
AFFAIR

Harmony Quartet – **ROSE** *and* **ONE OTHER GIRL** *and* **TWO BOYS.**

RUMOURS BUZZ ALONG THE WIRE
IS VIRGINIA RAPPÉ A LIAR?
SHE'S PUT FATTY IN THE FIRE
IT'S NINETEEN-TWENTY-THREE

The **COMPANY** *enters. The number takes us into the party.*

COMPANY
CLARA BOW'S THE LATEST HIT
SHE'S INVENTED A THING CALLED "IT"
DOROTHY PARKER'S INVENTED WIT
IT'S NINETEEN-TWENTY-FOUR

GUY LOMBARDO'S ALL THE RAGE
SARAH BERNHARDT'S LEFT THE STAGE
CECIL BEATON'S COME OF AGE
IT'S NINETEEN-TWENTY-FIVE

THURBER'S SMART NEW YORKER JOKES
SCOTT FITZGERALD'S WEEKEND SOAKS
READ THE LATEST HEADLINES FOLKS
IT'S NINETEEN-TWENTY-SIX

WHITE GIRL MARRIES HARLEM HIGH-KICKER
HEIRESS JAILED FOR CONTRABAND LIQUOR
HOLD IT MAN LET'S SEE WHAT THE TICKER
TAPE HAS GOT

Shouting.
THIS IS WHAT
BIG SENSATION IN NEW YORK
"FILM PRODUCERS GIVE A SQUAWK"
SILENT MOVIES START TO TALK

ACT II

IT'S NINETEEN TWENTY-SEVEN

COMPANY *routine.*

WHEN AL JOLSON BEATS THE DRUM
HOLLYWOOD BEGINS TO HUM
CALIFORNIA HERE THEY COME
THE TALKIES ARE AT THE GATE
IT'S NINETEEN-TWENTY-EIGHT

IT'S NINETEEN-TWENTY—
NINETEEN-TWENTY—
NINETEEN-TWENTY-EIGHT.

The **COMPANY** *break the line. There is party chatter.*

LILLIAN *and* **SENNETT** *enter.* **ROSE** *goes to greet them.*

ROSE Lillian... Mack... I'm so glad you could...

LILLIAN Rose, have you seen Mr Griffith?

ROSE No, but he's coming tonight.

LILLIAN Are you sure, Rose?

ROSE He promised me. And he never breaks his word...

GRIFFITH *enters.*

LILLIAN *and* **SENNETT** *move away, just missing* **GRIFFITH**.

Oh D.W., I knew you'd come.

GRIFFITH *(kissing* **ROSE***)* Is this the same party I was at last year or did you stop somewheres in between?

ROSE Ask me a question I can answer.

GRIFFITH OK ...have you heard what they're saying about me?

The party chatter rises and falls.

ROSE You know me. Never listen to gossip.

GRIFFITH They're saying I'm out-of-touch.

ROSE Who's "they", Mr Griffith?

GRIFFITH Mary and the money-men.

ROSE And what about your audience?

GRIFFITH Them I understand.

ROSE But do they understand you?

GRIFFITH They...

ROSE Do they come to your pictures? Are you giving them what they want?

GRIFFITH Who knows what they want?

ROSE I guess they do. What do *you* want?

GRIFFITH Just to make pictures. I've a head full of ideas.

ROSE New ones?

GRIFFITH I want to make a history of the world.

ROSE Oh.

GRIFFITH A heroic conception. To promote the League of Nations.

> **ZUKOR** *enters and crosses in front of* **GRIFFITH** *to* **SENNETT**.

ZUKOR Mack!

SENNETT Adolph!

ZUKOR Say, you heard about Warners'? They're planning to do an all-talking picture... Hello, D.W..

> **ZUKOR** *and* **SENNETT** *move away.*

ROSE Does it have to be that big?

GRIFFITH I write in fire and lightning. What do I want with small ideas?

ROSE Your audience might want them. Once in a while.

GRIFFITH Novelty. That's all they seem to look for these days.

ROSE And they get it in plenty from...

GRIFFITH Who?

ROSE Mr de Mille.

GRIFFITH All he ever photographs is Miss Swanson's bathroom.

ROSE People like something "peppy", Mr Griffith. Like Valentino.

GRIFFITH American men despised him.

ROSE American women didn't. He had "bedroom eyes".

GRIFFITH I have no ambition to make a picture about a man with bedroom eyes.

ROSE No...no, of course you don't.

GRIFFITH I shall film my history of the world.

ROSE So – you'll be needing money.

GRIFFITH Unfortunately.

VOICE *(offstage)* Mary!

There is a stir upstage.

ROSE Hey...I've got an idea. Just stick around. *(She moves upstage)* Ladies and gentlemen, positions please.

MARY *appears at the top of the steps in a long feathered cloak.*

I think you all know my guest of honour.

MARY *lets the cloak fall from her shoulders to reveal a stunning party dress.*

MARY Well...if I'd known, I'd have dressed for the occasion.

MUSIC 18: "THE BIOGRAPH GIRL"

COMPANY *(singing)*
SEE THAT SASSY DAME OF HIGH DEGREE

TAKES AWAY YOUR BREATH TO THINK THAT SHE
ONCE WAS
THE BIOGRAPH GIRL

MARY *(speaking)* One, two, three, four, five, six, seven, eight.

COMPANY *(singing)*
THERE'S NO DOUBT THAT SHE'S COME QUITE A WAY
SINCE THOSE DAYS IN NINETEEN-TWELVE WHEN THEY
CALLED HER THE BIOGRAPH GIRL

MARY *(speaking)* One, two, three, four, five, six, seven, eight.

COMPANY *(singing)*
SHE HOLDS THE KEY
TO ALL THE MOST IMPORTANT DOORS
AND BOY DOES SHE DRAW BLOOD (WOW!)
WHEN SHE DISPLAYS HER CLAWS

DISCUSSING MOVIE CONTRACTS SHE'S UNBEATABLE
IN A DEAL SHE'S UNDEFEATABLE
YES SIR SHE USED TO BE LESS SIR

IF THEY COULD SEE HER NOW THEY'D ALL REFUSE TO
    BELIEVE THIS FEMALE POWERHOUSE USED TO BE
LITTLE MARY
THE BIOGRAPH GIRL

MARY	COMPANY
IF EVER A GIRL	OOH
(speaking) Was lucky that girl was me	*(singing)* THE BIOGRAPH
God gave me the sense	OOH
To ask for the maximum fee	
	THE BIOGRAPH
Whenever I pose	
The cameras snap	OOH
A million dollars	
Fall into my lap	

COMPANY

ACT II

NO WONDER WE FOLLOW HER

MARY
THEY FOLLOW ME LIKE
THEY FOLLOW THEIR A.B.C.

I WALK DOWN THE STREET
AND ALL I CAN SEE IS ME

THEY'RE FOLLOWING ME
WHEN I'M DROPPING MY
   HEM
THEY'RE FOLLOWING ME
BUT I'M LOOKING LIKE
   THEM

COMPANY
OOH

THE BIOGRAPH
OOH

THE BIOGRAPH

OOH

COMPANY
THAT'S THE BIOGRAPH GIRL

SHE HOLDS THE KEY
TO ALL THE MOST IMPORTANT DOORS
AND BOY DOES SHE DRAW BLOOD (WOW!)
WHEN SHE DISPLAYS HER CLAWS

DISCUSSING MOVIE CONTRACTS SHE'S UNBEATABLE
IN A DEAL SHE'S UNDEFEATABLE
YES SIR SHE USED TO BE LESS SIR
IF THEY COULD SEE HER NOW THEY'D ALL REFUSE TO
   BELIEVE
THIS FEMALE POWERHOUSE USED TO BE
LITTLE MARY
THE BIOGRAPH GIRL

Dance.

ONE, TWO, THREE, FOUR
ONCE SHE USED TO LIVE ON CHARITY
NOW THIS LADY'S POPULARITY
RATING
IS DOLLAR-CREATING

Dance.

NO
ONE
ELSE
BUT
MARY
MARY
MARY - THE BIOGRAPH GIRL

After the number, the **COMPANY** *gather around* **MARY**. **ROSE** *crosses to* **GRIFFITH**, *who has been sitting watching.*

ROSE Well, there she is. Go and ask her. You created her, she'll listen to you.

GRIFFITH Mary?

ROSE Who else?

GRIFFITH Now?

ROSE Yes, now.

ROSE leaves him and GRIFFITH crosses to the others.

GRIFFITH Mary!

MARY *(from inside the group)* I know that voice.

The group clears. **MARY** *and* **GRIFFITH** *embrace.*

GRIFFITH Mary, I want to talk to you.

MARY And I want to talk to you too.

During the scene **LILLIAN** *stands in the wings to overhear their conversation.*

GRIFFITH What do you want to talk about, Mary – movies?

MARY No, David – money.

GRIFFITH I'm not too clever on that subject.

MARY Well I am. Now listen, and listen good... If we're going to stay in business together we need to modernize. In every department.

GRIFFITH I concede the need to streamline expenditure, but...

MARY Not just expenditure. Everything. Sets, scripts and stories.

GRIFFITH And how do you streamline a story?

MARY Simple. You cut out the bumf.

GRIFFITH You sound like a flapper, Mary.

MARY Good. They're our best customers.

GRIFFITH I don't speak their language. You'd better translate.

MARY Bumf is unnecessary detail. Like morals.

GRIFFITH The moral's what it's all about.

MARY The profit's what it's all about. It's the first lesson of business.

GRIFFITH I thought we were in the business of art.

MARY *(almost mocking)* The Universal Language?

GRIFFITH Something like that.

MARY The trip beyond Babel? To end war forever? We've just had the biggest war in history in case you didn't notice.

GRIFFITH Just because people won't listen to what I'm...

MARY Come on, David. It didn't work, did it? It didn't work. But United Artists is going to work. It's going to work if it kills me.*(She pauses)*. Or you.

There is a pause.

GRIFFITH I'm worried, Mary. Frankly – very worried.

MARY Oh?

GRIFFITH This manic search for novelty...it's a temporary thing. Where's it going to end? Where's it going to finish up? – you tell me that.

MARY Read *Variety*. Everybody else is.

GRIFFITH The talkies?! You can't be serious!

MARY Talkies are the future. And the sooner we face up to it the better.

GRIFFITH No, Mary, no.

MARY Yes, David. *(She pauses)* Yes.

GRIFFITH I will not make a talking picture. I don't deal in words. *(almost to himself)* It puts us back to Babel.

MARY Biblical epics are finished... Bib Pix Nix.

GRIFFITH You know I don't mean that. You know I... Do you realize how few people in the world speak English?

MARY I'm not so hot at it myself.

GRIFFITH If we make pictures that talk we can't send them round the world. It's suicide.

MARY No words, no pictures, Mr Griffith. It's as simple as that.

GRIFFITH Mary... *(coming closer)* Mary, I want to do a life of Lincoln.

MARY *(choking on her drink)* Abraham Lincoln? ...I thought you wanted to do a history of the world.

GRIFFITH *(disregarding her)* I've read a poem, Mary. Called *John Brown's Body*. I want to film a poem.

MARY Mr Griffith, are you crazy? You can't film a poem.

GRIFFITH I've done it before.

MARY *(losing her patience)* Oh, that was back in the Dark Ages. When people'd watch anything.

GRIFFITH This poem here won the Pulitzer Prize, Mary.

MARY So who's Pulitzer? And who the hell's John Brown?

GRIFFITH Mary...

MARY Look – poems are words, aren't they?

GRIFFITH Usually.

MARY *(very suspiciously)* Even ones that win Pulitzer Prizes?

GRIFFITH Especially those.

MARY Then the talkies were invented just for you!

GRIFFITH But...

MARY D.W., for the Prophet of the Silent Screen you make a hell of a lot of noise.

There is a pause.

GRIFFITH OK... OK, you win... I'll do a talkie. I'll do my life of Lincoln and I'll have him speak... And I'll keep a team of surgeons standing by so we can revive him after he's been assassinated and have a happy ending. *(He raises his glass to her)* The industry!

MARY *(raising her glass)* The industry...and us! *(quietly)* Do you know who I saw this morning? Lillian. The latest star to twinkle in Metro's galaxy... Why did you let her go?

GRIFFITH I... I didn't want to stand in her way.

MARY Come on, D.W..

GRIFFITH *(putting his glass down)* For all these years I've only seen one thing: watch the horizon...keep right on, boy...aim for that spot there, eyes right ahead. I never knew there was anything else but that horizon. I didn't realize what a prize I had in her until she was gone.

MARY *(taking his arm)* We're the same, you and me. Oh, I know you dream dreams and I dream dollar bills, but that's script detail when all's said and done. We've got blinkers on, the both of us. Like racehorses. Thoroughbreds, of course.

There is a pause.

GRIFFITH Mary, I do miss her.

MARY Well, of course you do. She was your whole life.

There is a pause.

GRIFFITH What?

MARY The best of you, the best of me – all mixed up in a package called Lillian Gish.

GRIFFITH My whole life?

MARY She meant the world to you. You know she did.

GRIFFITH *(easing away from* MARY*)* Mary, I'm afraid you've got it wrong. I didn't mean it that way at all.

MARY I thought you...

GRIFFITH She understood the way I work. She knew what to do without my even asking. She was the Griffith Heroine, Mary. It's that I miss.

MARY Then I feel sorry for you.

> MARY *exits.*

> *We realize that* LILLIAN *has been standing in the wings.*

> *The* COMPANY *exits to leave* LILLIAN *and* GRIFFITH *alone.*

LILLIAN Hello.

GRIFFITH Hello, Lillian. I'm going to make a talkie.

LILLIAN Oh, I'm glad. So very glad.

GRIFFITH Don't be, it means I've failed. I need the money. I'll be paying off for the rest of my life, Lillian. Life as it is has got me, after all.

LILLIAN How can you say that, Mr Griffith?

GRIFFITH I had a dream. But it never came true.

LILLIAN What does that mean?

GRIFFITH I don't know.

LILLIAN I know every movie I see's got your name written through it like a stick of candy. Isn't that enough for you?

GRIFFITH They're not *my* movies.

ACT II 75

LILLIAN They could be. If you'd just try to fit in. *(She pauses)* Look, where are you living?

GRIFFITH What does it matter?

LILLIAN I've been trying to reach you for the last two weeks.

GRIFFITH In a hotel. I said: it doesn't matter.

LILLIAN Hotels, Mr Griffith! Put some roots down.

GRIFFITH And what would I do with roots?

LILLIAN Feel more secure.

GRIFFITH *laughs.*

No, I mean it. You can't know until you've tried, and you've never done it, have you, Mr Griffith? You've never put yourself first. It's always been your reality or your truth or your dream or your journey. But never you. Just you.

GRIFFITH I wouldn't know how.

LILLIAN Then you're right – you have failed. You – of all people – just can't see.

There is a pause.

GRIFFITH Well, Miss Lillian...you're going to tell me, so I'd better ask. What is it...What is it I just can't see?

LILLIAN Your own success.

GRIFFITH *scoffs.*

No, hear me out. You had a dream, all right. A fool's dream, maybe, about love and things people don't want to speak too much of now – but a dream all the same. A shadow...

GRIFFITH Lillian...

LILLIAN Like a negative. Not in use at the moment. Put away in tissue paper.

GRIFFITH Lillian, what *is* this?

LILLIAN It's the future. Wrapped up and waiting for a better time.

GRIFFITH There isn't going to be one. I'm not God, Miss Lillian. I over-reached myself.

LILLIAN Open your eyes, Mr Griffith. See things.

GRIFFITH No.

LILLIAN Your ears too. Listen.

GRIFFITH Don't preach at me – no.

LILLIAN Listen to what they'll say about you. In ten years... twenty...fifty. That you were an inventor. That you were an artist. That you were a pioneer.

GRIFFITH *(raising his glass)* You're a good man, D.W.. Posterity's going to thank you.

LILLIAN *(quietly)* You're impossible.

> LILLIAN *exits but remains in the wings to watch* GRIFFITH.

GRIFFITH Miss Lillian...

MUSIC 19: "ONE OF THE PIONEERS"

Ten years? Twenty? Fifty? ...Maybe you're right at that, Miss Gish... The David Wark Griffith Tribute Dinner. What cliché will they not use?

Singing.
HE WAS ONE OF THE PIONEERS
A MAN WHO SWEPT ASIDE THE YEARS
AND TRAVELLED ON TILL THE FUTURE STRODE BESIDE HIM

HE WAS ONE OF THE PIONEERS
A MAN WHO CONQUERED HIS DOUBTS AND FEARS
WITH ONLY LOVE AND GOD ABOVE TO GUIDE HIM

OH YES HE KNEW OF LOVE
DON'T EVER DOUBT IT

HE TOOK THE VIEW OF LOVE
THAT NOTHING WORTHWHILE EVER GOT DONE WITHOUT IT

HE WAS ONE OF THE INNOVATORS
A FIRST INVENTOR AND NOW THE LATEST
TO GIVE THE WORLD A MILLION NEW CAREERS
CREATING SHADOWS BENEATH THE SUN
A GODDAM DREAMER WHO GOT THINGS DONE
SO LET US SALUTE HIM
HE WAS ONE OF THE PIONEERS

HE WAS ONE OF THE PIONEERS
A MAN WHO SWEPT ASIDE THE YEARS
AND TRAVELLED ON TILL THE FUTURE STRODE BESIDE HIM

HE WAS ONE OF THE PIONEERS
A MAN WHO CONQUERED HIS DOUBTS AND FEARS
WITH ONLY LOVE AND GOD ABOVE TO GUIDE HIM

OH YES HE KNEW OF LOVE
DON'T EVER DOUBT IT
HE TOOK THE VIEW OF LOVE
THAT NOTHING WORTHWHILE EVER GOT DONE WITHOUT IT

HE WAS ONE OF THE INNOVATORS
A FIRST INVENTOR AND NOW THE LATEST
TO GIVE THE WORLD A MILLION NEW CAREERS
CREATING SHADOWS BENEATH THE SUN
A GODDAM DREAMER...

GRIFFITH *can't carry on. He makes his exit.*

LILLIAN *comes on from the wings.*

SENNETT *appears at the back of the stage.*

LILLIAN Mack!

SENNETT Lillian! You haven't said a word to me all night long.

They sit on the steps together.

LILLIAN *(laughing)* You've been too busy. Spreading yourself around like peanut butter.

SENNETT I've got to, Lillian. It's times like this you need your friends.

LILLIAN Times like what?

SENNETT Come on – you know the business.

LILLIAN You're not worried about the talkies, Mack? Not you?

SENNETT So who wants a slapstick comic who speaks?

There is a silence.

There you are – even you don't have the answer.

MARY *and* ROSE *enter.*

ROSE Mary, you can't go yet.

MARY I've got to. I've the Louis Mountbattens for luncheon tomorrow.

LILLIAN Who'd've believed it? Royalty to lunch – with little Gladys Smith!

MARY *and* ROSE *sit on the steps.*

MARY Gladys Smith! ...Oh Lillian – boy, do we go back. *(to* SENNETT*)* Did she... *(laughing)* Did she ever tell you, Mack? She didn't even want to be in flickers.

LILLIAN Oh Mary, don't.

MARY Rose was there, she'll back me up. What was that movie I'd just made?

LILLIAN Ducks or something.

ROSE Geese.

ALL *Lena and the Geese*!

They laugh together.

MARY They came on the roof to rescue me.

ROSE But they stayed.

LILLIAN Dear Momma. It took her such a long time to accept it all.

There is a pause.

SENNETT I *wanted* to be in flickers.

LILLIAN *(laughing)* Do you remember your test?

SENNETT Remember it?

LILLIAN You pulled all those faces and he said you weren't real.

ROSE He was a good man.

MARY Who?

ROSE Griffith.

LILLIAN He still is.

The laughter has stopped.

SENNETT It's been sixteen years.

MARY Never. I don't feel a day over twelve.

VOICES *(offstage)* 'Bye, Rosie. Lovely party.

ROSE 'Scuse me, darlings... *(calling off)* So glad you could come.

ROSE *exits.*

MARY, **LILLIAN** *and* **SENNETT** *are alone.*

MARY At least he had his dreams – Mr Griffith.

LILLIAN You had yours too.

MARY Dollar bills aren't dreams. They can't even buy them.

LILLIAN All the same...

MARY I'm not a goddess, Lillian. Just a girl who got above herself. *(Pause)* Who said a career's just a beam of light?

SENNETT I think you did, Mary.

MARY Ever feel the light's getting dim, Mack?

SENNETT The candle always flickers. Before it goes out.

MUSIC 20: "PUT IT IN THE TISSUE PAPER"

Singing.
IN SIXTEEN SUCCESSFUL AND FAMOUS YEARS
I NEVER EVER THOUGHT
THE WORLD AND I
WOULD WAVE GOODBYE
TO THE SENNETT COMEDY SHORT
FROM *RASTUS AND THE GAME COCK*
TO THOSE CRAZY KEYSTONE KOPS

(speaking) Is this where the story stops?

ALL *(singing)*
PUT IT IN THE TISSUE PAPER
THEY WON'T WANT THAT SHADOW TILL ANOTHER DAY
WILL WE BE REISSUED LATER
OR CONDEMNED FOR LIFE UPON A SHELF TO STAY?

MARY *(singing)*
IN SIXTEEN SUCCESSFUL AND FAMOUS YEARS
MY INNOCENT PUBLIC FACE
HAS ALWAYS BEEN
ON THE SILVER SCREEN
IN THE FIRST AND FOREMOST PLACE
AND NOW AS THE SWEETHEART OF THE WORLD
MY IMAGE HAS REACHED ITS PEAK

(speaking) Is this where I have to speak?

ALL *(singing)*
PUT IT IN THE TISSUE PAPER
THEY WON'T WANT THAT SHADOW TILL ANOTHER DAY
WILL WE BE RE-ISSUED LATER
OR CONDEMNED FOR LIFE UPON A SHELF TO STAY?

LILLIAN *(singing)*
IN SIXTEEN SUCCESSFUL AND FAMOUS YEARS
I FOLLOWED WHERE HE LED
I DREAMED HIS DREAMS

BUT NOW IT SEEMS
THAT ALL THOSE DREAMS ARE DEAD
AND WHAT OF THE GOLDEN PROMISES
ALL THE GESTURES THAT WE MADE
IS THIS WHERE THE SHADOWS FADE?

ALL *(singing)*
PUT IT IN THE TISSUE PAPER
THEY WON'T WANT THAT SHADOW TILL ANOTHER DAY
WILL WE BE REISSUED LATER
OR CONDEMNED FOR LIFE UPON A SHELF TO STAY?

WHAT KIND OF SONG TO SING NOW
WHAT KIND OF WISH TO WISH NOW
WHAT KIND OF PRAYER TO PRAY NOW

TEACH US HOW TO SPEAK OH LORD
TEACH US ALL YOUR GOLDEN WORD
WHEN WE WALK WE DANCE
WHEN WE TALK WE SINGALONG

WE SING A SWAN SONG
OR WE DON'T SING AT ALL

PUT IT IN THE TISSUE PAPER

Fade to blackout.

Lights rise for the finale reprise with the **COMPANY** *on stage.*

MUSIC 21: "WORKIN' IN FLICKERS"

COMPANY
BACK WHEN GRIFFITH CAME OUT WEST
YOU SIGNED YOUR NAME AND TOOK A TEST
WE'D ALL OF US JUST BEGUN
WORKIN' IN FLICKERS

THINGS ARE DIFFERENT NOW FOR SURE
WE'RE USING SOUND AND WHAT IS MORE
WE DON'T NEED THE NOONDAY SUN
WORKIN' IN FLICKERS

WHEN THE TALKIES ARRIVED

WE HAILED A NEW REVOLUTION
IF YOU COME FROM THE BRONX
YOU'D BETTER TAKE ELOCUTION

SO MOVIES ARE BIG BUSINESS NOW
HEY - FOX IS LISTED ON THE DOW
AND BOX OFFICE IS THE THING
NOW LOUIS B IS KING
WE'RE ALL BREAKING BRAND NEW GROUND
THOUGH WE'RE MAKING A GREAT DEAL OF SOUND

WORKIN' IN FLICKERS

Music continues **LILLIAN** *steps forward.*

LILLIAN Little did we know that our smalltime flickers would be the foundation of something truly lasting. When sound was added to images, Mr Griffith's vision was realised in a way even he hadn't imagined possible. Film took its place alongside painting and music and theatre and dance as Art - Art in its own right. We in those silent pictures had taken the first faltering steps in what would be a march of enchantment and a journey of revolution.

SINCE THE TALKIES ARRIVED
WE'VE CERTAINLY SEEN SOME CHANGES
IF YOU HAPPEN TO SING
THEY WANT TO KNOW WHAT YOUR RANGE IS

FOR SIXTEEN YEARS WE SAW IT THROUGH
TO BRING THE PICTURE SHOW TO YOU
NO NEGATIVES - JUST A PLUS
WE HATE TO MAKE A FUSS
BUT BROTHER THAT WAS US

WORKIN' IN FLICKERS
WORKIN' IN FLICKERS
WORKIN' IN FLICKERS

Bows.

FURNITURE AND PROPERTY LIST

ACT I

On stage: Two permanent wooden "towers" left and right
Short flight of steps centre
Silent movie posters to be seen after *"OVERTURE"*

Offstage: Chimney pots ⎫ cut-outs (**CAST**)
Skylight ⎭
Chair (**CAST**)
Camera (**BITZER**)
Lens (**BITZER**)
Sack of letters (**MARY**)
Map (**ROSE**)
Chair, circle of Paramount stars (**MINIONS**)
Shoes (**LILLIAN**)
Desk – for Zukor (**CAST**)
Huge picture of Mary (to be flown)
Fur coat – for Mary (**CAST**)
Drawing board (**SPEC**)

Personal: **LADIES OF THE CHORUS:** pocket books
MARY: contract
GRIFFITH: shoe with hole in sole

ACT II

Onstage: As **ACT I** except for movie posters
Two advertising boards announcing "Intolerance—Trade Preview"

Offstage: Notepad (**ROSE**)
Cocktail Bar with cocktails—for **ROSE**'s party (**CAST**)

LIGHTING PLOT

Only essential cues are listed here
Permanent set representing many locations

ACT I

To open: General lighting

Cue 1	After *"OVERTURE"* *Change to faint flickering blue.*	(Page 1)
Cue 2	After *"MUSIC 1(A)"* *Revert to previous lighting.*	(Page 1)
Cue 3	As *"MUSIC 3"* starts *Concentrate light on* **MARY**.	(Page 3)
Cue 4	**MARY** exits *Lights up on Biograph Studio rooftop.*	(Page 4)
Cue 5	**GRIFFITH**: "Somehow I think we will." *Change of light for fight.*	(Page 13)
Cue 6	**GRIFFITH**: "…and Hollywood." *Change lights.*	(Page 14)
Cue 7	During *"MUSIC 5"* *"Griffith Wipe" effect on cyclorama.*	(Page 15)
Cue 8	At end of *"MUSIC 6"* *Blackout.*	(Page 20)
Cue 9	When ready *Lights up.*	(Page 21)
Cue 10	**GRIFFITH**: "…a whole army and then some!" *Lights dim to single spot on* **ROSE**.	(Page 31)
Cue 11	Company unfreeze for *"MUSIC 9"* *Revert to general lighting.*	(Page 33)
Cue 12	At end of *"MUSIC 9"* *Blackout.*	(Page 35)

Cue 13   When ready   (Page 35)
          Lights up to normal.

ACT II

To open: Darkness

Cue 14   When ready   (Page 49)
          Single spot on **ROSE**.

Cue 15   **ROSE**: "...blinking of an eye."   (Page 49)
          Lights expand to whole stage.

Cue 16   At end of*"MUSIC 14(A)"*   (Page 56)
          Blackout.

Cue 17   When ready   (Page 56)
          Single spots extreme left and right.

Cue 18   **ROSE**: "Hollywood. Just Hollywood."   (Page 57)
          Lights expand to reveal **COMPANY**.

Cue 19   During *"MUSIC 15"*   (Page 61)
          Slow fade to single spot on **GRIFFITH**.
          Fade spot at end of song.

Cue 20   When ready   (Page 62)
          General lights up on **ROSE** *and* **MARY**.

THIS IS NOT THE END

Visit samuelfrench.co.uk and discover the best theatre bookshop on the internet

A vast range of plays
Acting and theatre books
Gifts

samuelfrench.co.uk
samuelfrenchltd
samuel french uk

Lightning Source UK Ltd.
Milton Keynes UK
UKHW02f0607210518
322897UK00005B/77/P